Snapshots of the Past

"Thus the sum of things is ever being renewed, and mortals live dependent one upon another. Some races increase, others diminish, and in a short space the generations of living creatures are changed and like runners hand on the torch of life."

Lucretius, *de Rerum Natura*, II, 75
(Translated by Cyril Bailey)

Snapshots of the Past

BRIAN FAGAN

ALTAMIRA
PRESS

A Division of
ROWMAN & LITTLEFIELD PUBLISHERS, INC.
Walnut Creek • Lanham • New York • Oxford

ACC LIBRARY SERVICES
AUSTIN, TX

ALTAMIRA PRESS
A Division of Rowman & Littlefield Publishers, Inc.
1630 North Main Street, #367
Walnut Creek, CA 94596
www.altamirapress.com

Rowman & Littlefield Publishers, Inc.
A wholly owned subsidiary of the Rowman & Littlefield Publishing Group
4501 Forbes Boulevard, Suite 200
Lanham, MD 20706

PO Box 317, Oxford, OX2 9RU, UK

Copyright © 1995 by AltaMira Press
Interior Design and Production: Labrecque Publishing Services

British Library Cataloguing in Publication Information Available

Library of Congress Cataloging-in-Publication Data

Fagan, Brian M.
    Snapshots of the past/Brian Fagan
      p. cm
    Includes bibliographical references (p.).
    ISBN 978-0-7619-9109-0
    1. Human evolution. 2. Fossil man. 3. Man, Prehistoric.
I. Title.
GN281.F355 1995
573.3—dc20   95-32478

Printed in the United States of America

♾™ The paper used in this publication meets the minimum requirements of American National Standard for Information Sciences—Permanence of Paper for Printed Library Materials, ANSI/NISO Z39.48–1992.

ABOUT THE AUTHOR

B rian Fagan studied archaeology and anthropology at Pembroke College, Cambridge, and spent his early career in tropical Africa, where he studied the Iron Age cultures of Central Africa. Since 1967, he has been Professor of Anthropology at the University of California, Santa Barbara, and has specialized in public archaeology. A well-known lecturer and writer, he has written many general books on archaeology, including *Time Detectives* (Simon & Schuster, New York, 1995) and *The Adventure of Archaeology* (National Geographic Society, Washington D.C., 1984). His textbooks on archaeology, *In the Beginning* (8th edition, 1993), *People of the Earth* (8th edition, 1994), and *Archaeology: A Brief Introduction* (5th edition, 1993) (all HarperCollins, New York), are widely used in many parts of the world. 🌞

Sites Mentioned in the Book

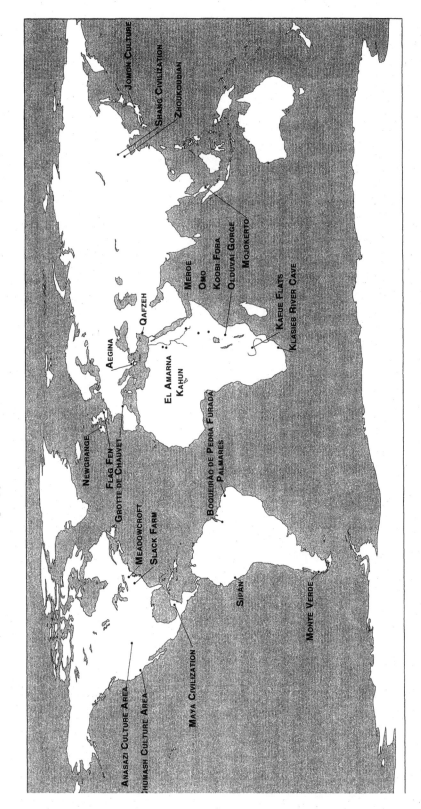

PREFACE

The articles in this book were originally published as bimonthly "Timelines" columns in *Archaeology Magazine*. By its very nature, a magazine column ranges widely over many subjects, seeking to entertain, inform, and sometimes wax indignant. "Timelines" explored the first settlement of the Americas, the ethics of professional archaeologists, Pacific navigation, and Bronze Age woodwork. I wrote about the scandalous looting of the Slack Farm site in Kentucky, lamented the crowds of tourists thronging Greek temples, and praised the work of the Archaeological Conservancy. We visited Cecil B. De Mille's *The Ten Commandments* movie set in California, traced archaic humans from Africa to Asia, and showed how Chinese civilization could be dated by eclipses.

While working on the columns, I was amazed and delighted by the fascinating byways of archaeology, many of them unknown to a wider audience. Modern archaeological research is highly specialized and often extremely esoteric. People forge careers out of an expertise with prehistoric earthworms or isotopic analysis of human bone. Today's archaeology is a far cry from the small armies of workers who labored under Victorian archaeologists at Nineveh or Troy, with as much research being conducted in the laboratory and with the microscope as in the field. Each specialty has its own jargon, its own cultural terms and artifact terminologies. So the "Timelines" columns navigated through the maze of detail and specialized literature, creating snapshots of archaeology, archaeologists, and our complex, multifaceted past. A selection of them appears in these pages.

Acknowledgements

The author and publisher gratefully acknowledge the cooperation of *Archaeology Magazine*, especially its editor, Peter Young. These articles first appeared in the magazine's "Timelines" columns in the following issues:

Aping the Apes	May/June 1992
Elusive *Homo Erectus*	July/August 1994

The author also wishes to thank Clare Tuffy, manager of Newgrange, and her colleagues; Ruth Moran and Brian Thornberry of the Irish Tourist Board; Charles E. Orser, Jr. of Illinois State University; Julie Ruiz-Sierra; David Pollack, Kentucky Heritage Council; Cheryl Ann Munson, Indiana University, Bloomington; and Stephen Houston, Brigham Young University, for their assistance with various articles appearing in this book. ☀

TABLE OF CONTENTS

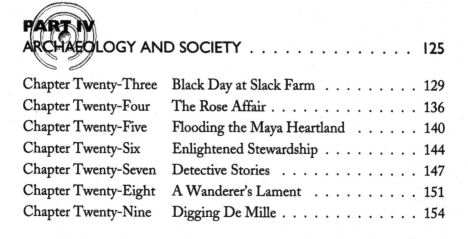

INTRODUCTION

The adventure of archaeology began with the heroic discoveries of adventurers and professional travelers in the nineteenth century. John Lloyd Stephens and Frederick Catherwood revealed the glories of ancient Maya civilization to an astonished world in the 1840s. They were not archaeologists, but made their living with pen and brush for an armchair audience captivated by high adventure. The German archaeologist Heinrich Schliemann made a fortune from the California Gold Rush, then retired from business to discover Homeric Troy in northwest Turkey in 1871. Self-educated and determined, Schliemann loved the romance and excitement of archaeological discovery. At no point in his career could he be described as a trained archaeologist. He even employed engineers from the Suez Canal to supervise his vast excavations. Just before World War I, British archaeologist Leonard Woolley excavated the Hittite city of Carchemish on the Euphrates River in Syria. He worked with a crowd of unruly workers and did not hesitate to draw his revolver on stubborn officials. Charismatic and forceful, Woolley was the epitome of the archaeologist of yesteryear. A digger and scholar, he was a jack-of-all-trades, as adept at deciphering a cuneiform tablet as he was at excavating a royal cemetery.

The days of the Schliemanns and Woolleys are long gone, remembered today only in the famed Indiana Jones movies, which depict their hero as a swashbuckling, flamboyant adventurer. Bullwhips and fedora hats do not the archaeologist make, however. While Indiana Jones himself is a fictional composite of many colorful Victorian archaeologists, he bears no resemblance to the archaeologist of today. For in the short span of a century, archaeology has turned from a romantic, casual adventure into a serious, multidisciplinary science. Even 50 years ago, only a few hundred professional archaeologists made up the archaeological family. Now there are thousands of us, working in universities and colleges, museums, government agencies, even in privately owned companies carrying out environmental assessments. The traditional stereotype of the pith-helmeted professor excavating in the shadow of great pyramids, or searching for golden pharaohs, is as dead as the dodo. Today's archaeologists are highly trained specialists, as comfortable behind a binocular microscope as in a trench in the field. They are anthropologists and historians, scientists and multidisciplinary scholars studying every chapter of human history from our origins more than 2.5 million years ago to early factories of the Industrial Revolution, even modern urban garbage.

Anthropologists study human beings as biological organisms and as people with a distinctive and unique characteristic—culture. Archaeologists are special kinds of anthropologists who study ancient societies, using the material remains of their lives. Unlike ethnologists, they cannot speak to their subjects, who are long dead. They study ancient human behavior, building theories and applying scientific techniques and theoretical concepts in examining the material remains of human culture. Some people think archaeology is little more than an assortment of techniques used to gather evidence from the soil. Modern archaeology is far more than a constellation of techniques, for it involves not only ordering and recording the archaeological record, but also interpreting and publishing the evidence from the earth. Archaeology is an interactive discipline, striking a balance between practical excavation and description, and theoretical interpretation.

No one can possibly be an expert in the entire span of archaeology, so most archaeologists specialize. Prehistoric archaeologists study prehistoric times, from human origins right up to the frontiers of documentary history, which began in Mesopotamia about 5,000 years ago. Classical archaeologists study the remains of the great Classical civilizations of Greece and Rome. There are Egyptologists and Assyriologists, experts on Etruscan civilization, on early Chinese states, scholars with remarkable expertise in archaeology and in ancient scripts. Many archaeologists who carry out document-aided research are historical archaeologists working on sites from historical periods. They dig deep into Medieval York in England, investigate Colonial villages, eighteenth-century New York, and frontier forts. Archaeologists work deep underwater studying ancient shipwrecks, investigate Biblical cities, even Victorian railroad stations. Some fieldworkers have lived for months on end with arctic caribou hunters or San foragers in southern Africa's Kalahari Desert, studying the dynamics of living societies still practicing traditional lifeways, collecting empirical data that can be used to interpret the archaeological record. Others are inveterate experimenters, replicating life in the past with controlled experiments. After months of toolmaking, one archaeologist has shown that some of the very first humans were left-handed. Others have felled trees with stone axes, blown replicas of the Egyptian pharaoh Tutankhamun's trumpets, and even deliberately burnt down precise replicas of ancient houses–to see what the foundations look like.

Whatever their specialties, all archaeologists are united by their common interest in studying humanity in the past. Whether they focus on the earliest humans or on those of recent times, they all agree that archaeology has three main goals:

- To study archaeological sites and their contents in a context of time and space, to describe long sequences of human culture,

- To reconstruct past lifeways, to deduce how humans made their livings, and

- To explain why human cultures changed, or why they remained the same, over long periods of time.

Many people think that archaeology is an expensive luxury in a world where grinding poverty and hunger are commonplace. Why, they ask, is it important to dig up and study the past? Archaeology is unique among all the sciences, as it is the only reliable way of studying and explaining how human societies have changed—or remained the same—over very long periods of time. Quite apart from studying our origins among the non-human primates, the long time frame of archaeology allows us to trace the origins of modern humanity, as well as to examine the beginnings of human diversity. If the geneticists and archaeologists are to be believed, our earliest modern ancestors evolved in tropical Africa between 200,000 and 100,000 years ago, making us, as Harvard biologist Stephen J. Gould has said, "products of the same common African twig." We live in an increasingly diverse industrial society, where people from diverse cultures are thrown in closer juxtaposition than ever before. Any means by which we can understand how the fundamental differences and similarities between us evolved is of cardinal importance. Archaeology gives us the long view, a unique chronicle of diversity from the frontiers of the Great Ice Age and even earlier.

Archaeology is a product of Western science, of a fundamental curiosity about the origins of humanity that goes back to Classical times, and even earlier. Westerners have a linear view of time, extending back more than 2.5 million years into the remote past. Archaeology espouses such a linear perspective, a landscape of the past peopled with cultures and societies that became increasingly complex as the centuries and millennia unfolded. This line-like view of the past is at odds with the cyclical view of time in which many non-Western societies flourish. Numerous native American societies measured the passage of time by the changing of the seasons, linking this to a symbolic view of life itself as a cycle of birth, life, and death. For example, the ancient Maya of Central America measured time by the passage of the heavenly bodies and thought of it in terms of great 52-year cycles, the transition from one to the next being marked by elaborate religious ceremonies. Such cyclical views of time, of human existence, place less importance on tracing remote human origins, on the view of history reconstructed by archaeology. Rather, the emphasis is on "being," on human existence, the reasonable expectation being that one's ancestors enjoyed the same life as one did, and that one's descendants will inherit the same existence. This cyclical perspective puts some native Americans and others on a philosophical collision course with archaeologists, with the former considering the latter subversive to the integrity of their culture. In many cases, however, native American groups and archaeologists ally with one another to preserve sacred sites and to save ancient settlements from destruction by looters or modern-day development.

Despite these fundamental, and often deeply felt, philosophical differences, archaeologists have a vital role to play in the writing of human history, using *history* in the fullest sense of the word. To many people, "history" means documents and dusty archives, the written records set down by heads of state and government officials, by men and women going about their daily round. But human history encompasses far more than the mere 5,000 years of documentary history. And even this 5,000-year figure applies only

14

to ancient Egypt and Mesopotamia. Continuous written records for parts of central Africa begin in A.D. 1890, when European colonial powers absorbed that continent into their vast empires. Many New Guinea groups first set foot on the stage of written history as recently as the 1950s and 1960s. In both areas, human occupation goes back tens of thousands, and in Africa millions of years, into the past. Both documents and oral histories, passed from one generation to the next, record but a tiny proportion of African or New Guinean history. Only archaeology provides the long chronological perspective, a means of reconstructing the complex histories of tribal groups, large and small, and of long-forgotten ancient African states. In many African schools and universities, history reconstructed with the spade forms a major part of the historical curriculum, a means of fostering cultural identity, or forging a multidimensional history of all humankind. Therein lies archaeology's most important contribution to human understanding: its ability to treat all societies evenly, to compare and contrast the humblest with the most elaborate, complex civilizations which flourished in widely separated parts of the world. Archaeology lies at the heart of a truly global history, divorced from the narrowly ethnocentric visions of the past which appear, even today, in so many history books, in schools and universities.

Archaeology encompasses all time periods, all lands. Archaeological sites everywhere, whether the mighty Pyramids of Giza, or a tiny scatter of stone tools in the heart of the Mojave Desert, are all part of the marvelous, common cultural heritage of all humankind. We have much to learn from the past, from our ancestors' ingenious ways of adapting to diverse natural environments, from their solutions to farming in cold regions, or to raising crops with simple technology, from their skills with crops, animals, and metals. We live with—even on—the precedents of history. Everywhere we turn, the forces of history are with us, encouraging, threatening, giving us perspectives on our own doings. We learn we are not the first to face poverty and war, to cope with drought or catastrophic epidemics. We learn that urban overcrowding was a problem in Sumerian Mesopotamia, that Egyptian students were lazy in the classroom. We can look back at the past and see our forebears wrestling with the common, day-to-day problems of life, just as we do. The archaeological sites of the world, and the knowledge we gain from them, are no one nation, or individual's, property. They belong to us all, for their are part of the collective fabric of human history, providing us with a vision of diversity and commonality in an increasingly crowded and challenging world. For this reason, we must preserve the monuments and settlements of the past for the future, so that our grandchildren can learn from those who have gone before, as we have done. To study archaeology is to study ourselves, diverse humankind.

The past, the archaeological record, is all around us, conspicuous and inconspicuous, something all of us encounter frequently in out lives, perhaps as landowners, or in construction work, or as tourists. Archaeology is for everybody to enjoy, for enjoying the past is one of the great pleasures of the modern world. The twentieth century has witnessed spectacular discoveries, which have transformed our knowledge of ancient times and helped turn archaeological tourism into a major global industry. From an early preoccupation with fossil humans and long-lost civilizations, archaeology has been transformed into a sophisticated multidisciplinary science which spans more than two-and-a-half million years of human history.

The articles reprinted in this volume are grouped into four broad themes:

- *The study of early lifeways.* Eight articles discuss early hunter-gatherers, hominids, and farmers,

- *Issues surrounding more complex early societies.* Concerned with document-aided research, these seven articles explore aspects of early civilization and recent historic societies.

- *Issues in contemporary archaeology.* Seven articles explore major controversies in archaeology,

- *Archaeology and society.* Archaeology is an integral part of contemporary society. These seven articles discuss some of the ways in which archaeology intersects with our own lives.

I wrote two articles specially for this book. The first, "Prehistoric Artists," explores the recent discovery of a painted cave in France and speculates about the meaning of such rock art in the context of what we know about prehistoric San art from southern Africa. The second, "The

16

Humbler Egyptians," discusses the lives of Egyptian townspeople in the Middle and New Kingdoms of Ancient Egypt, and explores their ties to their home villages.

I hope that these pages allow you to enjoy the past as much as I have. And may you, too, one day, have the experience of visiting the Pyramids of Giza at full moon, or listening to Greek stanzas echoing up the serried seats in the amphitheater at Epidauros on a spring evening. These are the experiences that make our forebears come alive for us all. ☼

PART I
EARLY LIFEWAYS

The great palaeoanthropologists Louis and Mary Leakey imprinted the study of human origins firmly on the public consciousness in the 1960s with their dramatic discoveries at Olduvai Gorge in East Africa. The Leakey family members became public figures through television specials and the pages of *National Geographic Magazine*. Louis Leaky in particular won fame as a colorful advocate of a multidisciplinary approach to human evolution. It was he who inspired Dian Fossey and Jane Goodall to spend years on end living among our closest living relatives, chimpanzees and gorillas. And it was Leakey who created a compelling portrait of our earliest ancestors as hunters and expert plant gatherers more than a million years ago. He proclaimed the scatters of stone choppers and flakes at Olduvai to be the actual campsites of early hominids. Leakey's vision survived for a generation, until younger scholars turned to the microscope and the study of carnivores to interpret the broken animal bones on the Olduvai "floors." "Aping the Apes" recounts how hi-tech science has revolutionized our knowledge of early hominid behavior, revealing it to be far more ape-like than human.

Our archaic ancestors of a million years ago or more will always be elusive because they were few in number, their toolkits simple and highly portable, and constantly on the move. "Elusive *Homo Erectus*" describes how scientists have recently overturned the dating for the first spread of archaic humans from tropical Africa, using dating techniques unimaginable a generation ago. "Prehistoric Artists" fast-forwards us to the time of the European Cro-Magnons, about 15,000 years ago, when the world was locked in the deep-freeze of the late Ice Age. We do not know exactly when humans first became artists, but there is reason to believe that people were engraving and painting cave and rockshelter walls in Europe, Australia, and Africa before 20,000 years ago. We describe the recent discovery of the Grotte de Chauvet in France and speculate about the motives for the earliest art traditions of all, using an analogy from the complex world of San art in

19

southern Africa. Which raises a question: what was it like to live in a world where game was abundant, where everyone lived off wild game and other gathered foods? "Reflections on the Kafue Flats" draws on my personal experience in Africa to dramatize the profound continuity between prehistoric hunter-gatherers and the few surviving foraging-groups of the twentieth-century world. The same article also introduces the potential of ethnoarchaeology, the study of living peoples and both their artifacts and their daily life as a means of interpreting the archaeological record.

The last four articles in Part I describe some of the changes in human society that resulted from profound global warming at the end of the Ice Age some 15,000 years ago. As temperatures rose and ice sheets retreated, the world's temperate environments changed beyond recognition. Hundreds of big-game species became extinct. The hunter-gatherer societies of the world adapted to new environmental realities by engaging in ever more specialized hunting and gathering, by fine-tuning their subsistence practices to local environments. In some favored areas of the world, hunter-gatherer groups settled down in permanent settlements, almost invariably in regions where fish were abundant. The Jomon fisherfolk of Japan were one such society, flourishing for thousands of years off a bounty of marine resources, only turning to agriculture as a supplement to their traditional diet when populations rose to high densities.

Agriculture began in many parts of the world, not as a brilliant invention, but rather as a means of supplementing the intensive foraging of wild cereal grasses or root crops. At the same time, hunters in the Old World began to experiment with the penning and taming of more tractable animals like the wild goat and sheep, and even the wild ox. The latter is a surprising choice, for the primordial aurochs (*Bos primigenius*) is a fierce and formidable beast, much feared by hunters armed with sophisticated weapons, let alone simple spears bows and arrows. "Taming the Aurochs" paints one possible scenario for the domestication of this intractable beast in the most unlikely of environments, the depths of the Sahara Desert.

Cro-Magnon cave art reflects the complex ideologies and beliefs that circumscribed ancient hunter-gatherer societies. Farmers, with their close links to the land, enjoyed equally complex ritual experiences. "Neolithic Newgrange" describes one of Europe's most spectacular religious monuments, a sacred burial chamber that enshrined revered ancestors and also served to commemorate the passage of the seasons—the cycles of birth (planting), life (maintaining), and death (harvesting) that governed the lives of ancient farming societies. The same article introduces another persistent theme in these columns: the many opportunities that exist to experience and enjoy the past, by studying the great archaeological sites of the world.

Finally, we explore the complex landscape created by late Bronze Age farmers at Flag Fen in eastern England. Some 3,000 years ago, they built an artificial platform in the midst of a swamp and connected it to higher ground with an irregular post alignment. In so doing, they created a veritable jigsaw of oak, alder, and other timbers that has defied the best efforts of archaeologists to reassemble it. Every field season yields a little more information, like the recent discovery of a wooden wheel and trackways close to the platform. Flag Fen offers a classic example of how cumulative field research over many seasons slowly builds up a changing picture of ancient life.

Part I explicates some of the remote foundations of the far more complex ancient world that developed over the past 5,000 years, described in the articles in Part II. ☀

CHAPTER ONE
APING THE APES

T he 1960s through the mid-1980s were years of epic early hominid discoveries at Olduvai Gorge in Tanzania, at East Turkana in Kenya, and at Hadar in Ethiopia. These were the years when human evolution became part of popular culture, when Louis and Mary Leakey, their son Richard, Donald Johanson, and others became celebrities. It was Louis Leakey who named the first human *Homo habilis*, "handy person," the first toolmaker. It was he who argued the scatters of broken bones and crude stone choppers in Bed I at Olduvai were all that was left of temporary encampments where *Homo habilis* butchered animals, ate, and slept in brush shelters nearly 2 million years ago. Leakey thought that the males did the hunting while the women foraged for wild plant foods—an idea based on Canadian anthropologist Richard Lee's work among the !Kung San, a modern hunter-gatherer group living in the Kalahari Desert of southern Africa. When Richard Leakey discovered more early humans at Koobi Fora in northern Kenya, this "man the hunter, woman the gatherer" model acquired even greater antiquity—at least 2.5 million years.

Although the Leakeys' portrait of *Homo habilis* was applauded by such eminent archaeologists as the late Glynn Isaac, it rapidly came under fire on the grounds that it was based on incomplete information. How had the scatters of bones and stone fragments been formed? Had they accumulated in a few days . . . even hours? Or were they the result of occasional visits over a long period of time?

The study of what are called "site-formation processes" is relatively new to archaeology. Richard Potts of the Smithsonian Institute has studied the Olduvai "floors" with meticulous care. He used geological evidence to establish that they were, indeed, not of natural origin. Potts examined the ways in which individual bones were fractured, both at their articular ends and along the shafts. He examined the different bones for telltale traces of

23

both carnivore and hominid damage to the same fragments. Potts believes that several agencies were at work in site formation at Olduvai. At least one presumed site was formed predominantly by carnivores; others, which have both artifacts and bones, resulted from hominids bringing tools and bones to the site. Judging from the weathering on individual bones, Potts estimates each "floor" accumulated over a period of about five years. He also believes that they were not campsites at all, but places where hominids cached stone flakes and cores. They used these places regularly when scavenging meat from nearby predator kills.

There are several arguments in favor of Potts's hypothesis. First, the bones and stones are concentrated in tight groupings and were deposited over a considerable period of time. Second, the transported bones bear cut-marks from stone tools. Third, many of the bones were never completely processed and were abandoned while still covered with meat and with marrow intact. Carnivore teeth marks on some of the bones are occasionally superimposed on stone tool cut-marks, as if hyenas and other animals visited the fresh accumulation after the hominids left. Last, the hominids left lumps of imported but unprocessed stone at the caches, as if they planned to return.

If Potts is right in thinking the Olduvai deposits were indeed stone caches, what about the early human lifeway itself? The animal bones from Olduvai come from a wide variety of species that once flourished near the shallow lake. Did *Homo habilis* actually hunt antelope and other animals, or did our earliest ancestors merely scavenge meat from lion and hyena kills?

Many experts now believe that *Homo habilis* scavenged meat from nearby predator kills, chasing away lions with stones and loud calls. The hominids would then grab choice pieces of meat and retreat to a convenient spot, perhaps under the shade of a tree, where they had already stashed stone flakes and raw materials. There they would eat the fresh meat, using flakes and stones to strip off the flesh and break up the bones for their marrow. Once their hunger was satisfied, they would move off, leaving the smashed bones for other predators to scavenge. The hominids would return to the same place on several occasions, perhaps because there was water nearby, or because a convenient tree provided both shelter and a place of refuge. We can assume, however, that their visits were sufficiently infrequent so that carnivores did not lie in wait for them.

The new research shows that our earliest ancestors behaved in a more ape-like than human manner, spending much of their life in the trees, even if they ventured onto the open savanna for meat and plant foods. They may have run down and hunted a few species of smaller animals, but, as far as we can tell, they hunted without spears. The lack of spears makes close-quarter stalking essential and fleetness of foot vital. It also means that hominids with an upright posture and the ability to run fast were well-equipped to scavenge meat from predator kills, moving in quickly, grabbing convenient body parts, and running away to safety in the shortest possible time. Without fire and spears, our earliest ancestors would have been vulnerable to sudden attack, especially at night. Most likely, then, they slept in trees and did not establish campsites in open country.

This much more ape-like portrait of *Homo habilis* has been pieced together from a patchwork of telling clues, some of them almost invisible to the naked eye. The new scenario raises a fundamental question about the evolution of human behavior. When did we first hunt big game, live in camps, share food, and become fully "human"?

New research is under way in Ethiopia, so ravaged by civil war and famine in the 1980s. Ethiopian scholars trained at the University of California at Berkeley are collaborating with American scientists on a long-term campaign of survey and excavation. This time they have the benefit of sophisticated satellite images that will enable them to plot the distribution of extensive fossil beds long before a single paleoanthropologist goes into the field—a method that is already paying off. Only a few months ago an international team unearthed some hominid teeth at Fejiji in an area where no fossils had ever been found—some 600 miles southwest of Hadar where Donald Johanson discovered Lucy more than a decade ago. Johanson and another team have returned to Hadar, and their first season has yielded the remains of 15 hominids between 3 and 3.5 million years old. They include an upper arm bone with such robust shoulder muscle attachments that the individual would have been able to swing with ease into the trees.

Perhaps the new finds at Hadar are another indication that our earliest ancestors were more ape-like than human in their behavior, that our humanness is, indeed, relatively recent. As Stephen J. Gould has written, and mitochondrial DNA may show, "We are all products of a recent African twig." Just how recent that twig is is only now becoming apparent. ☀

CHAPTER TWO
ELUSIVE HOMO ERECTUS

They sought it with thimbles,
  they sought it with care;
They pursued it with forks and hope;
They threatened its life with a
  railway share;
They charmed it with smiles and soap.

—Lewis Carroll, *The Hunting of the Snark*

Of all the early hominids, *Homo erectus* is the most elusive and puzzling, a "snark" of human paleontology. Compared to the hundreds of Australopithecine and early *Homo* fossils found by the Leakeys, Donald Johanson, and others in East Africa during the past 20 years, relatively few *Homo erectus* species have been discovered. Astonishingly, we know far more about our earliest ancestors than we do about their descendant. Perhaps we should say descendants, for there are now signs that *Homo erectus* was a more complex species than paleoanthropologists suspected. *Homo erectus* remains have been found throughout Southeast Asia and in North Africa, and some scholars believe the species thrived in Europe too, although this remains a topic of debate. What is sending shock waves throughout the paleoanthropological community, however, are the dates for these finds that new and improved techniques are yielding. It seems that *Homo erectus* left Africa much earlier than previously thought.

The story of *Homo erectus* began with an obsessive young Dutch physician named Eugene Dubois, who was convinced that the elusive missing link between apes and humans had flourished in the rain forests of

Southeast Asia. He took a post as a government doctor in fever-ridden Indonesia so he could search for human fossils. Although Dubois embarked on his quest with nothing but a hunch, months of searching were crowned with success. In 1890, he found his first human bones in central Java. The following year, he excavated a massive cranium from the gravels of Trinil on the slow-flowing Solo River. Some time later, he recovered a remarkably complete, modern-looking human femur from the same gravels. Dubois knew he had found something more primitive than the well-known Neanderthal skulls from Europe, a fossil much more likely to be a missing link. He named his Java hominid *Pithecanthropus erectus,* literally the Ape-Human who stood erect, and claimed it was a primitive human form close to the apes. The full fury of established science descended on Dubois's shoulders When he returned to the Netherlands. Rejected and discouraged, Dubois became a scientific recluse.

Thirty years later, however, Chinese and European scientists excavating the deep caves and fissures at Zhoukoudian near Beijing unearthed crania and other human bones bearing a remarkable similarity to those found by Dubois. Excavations continued at Zhoukoudian until the outbreak of World War II. Fortunately, the eminent anatomist Franz Weidenreich described the original fossils in great detail, for they were lost during the War. Since the 1930s, Dutch paleontologist Ralph von Koenigswald and others have found more *Homo erectus* fossils at sites on the Solo River and at Sangiran some 50 miles away. Today scientists classify all of these finds collectively as *Homo erectus,* a taxonomic recognition that they were a long evolutionary distance from apes or putative ape-humans.

What do we know about the physical characteristics of *Homo erectus?* They stood fully upright, and were nimble walkers and runners. Richard Leakey's discovery of the remains of a 12-year-old boy, five-feet-six-inches tall, at Lake Turkana in northern Kenya, suggests that *Homo erectus* males may have reached a height of six feet at maturity. Their hands were fully capable of precision gripping and many kinds of toolmaking, and their thick-walled skulls more rounded than those of earlier hominids. *Homo erectus* had a sloping forehead and head browridge that supported the muscles of its massive jaws. With a highly varied brain capacity between 800 and 1,300 cubic centimeters, these were humans who were capable of extensive thought and had excellent vision. We still do not know whether they were capable of fully articulate speech.

The earliest well-dated *Homo erectus* specimens came from the Lake Turkana region where their crania were potassium-argon dated to at least 1.8 million years ago. Dated initially by informed guesswork, the earliest of the Asian hominids were believed to be about 1 million years old, more recent than primordial African populations. Thus, the experts have argued *Homo erectus* evolved from earlier *Homo habilis* populations on the African savanna, then migrated out of Africa about a million years ago. Equipped with a new weapon—fire—*Homo erectus* groups soon populated temperate Europe, Southeast Asia, and China.

African *Homo erectus* was a hunter and a forager, well-adapted to open savanna grassland. Its Asian cousins lived in tropical forests, where game was rare and bamboo and wood resources were of vital importance. In 1948, the Harvard archaeologist Hallam Movius divided the world of *Homo erectus* into two vast provinces. In Africa and Europe were the hand-ax makers, people adapted to open country who used stone axes and cleavers (named after the northern French town of St. Acheul) to butcher animals large and small. In Asia the environment of woodland and forest required simpler choppers and other woodworking tools. Movius described Asia as an area of cultural retardation that never played "a vital and dynamic role in early human evolution." Archaeologists thought of this "chopper-chopping tool complex" as a backward culture based predominantly on bamboo that developed in isolation.

More recent interpretations, however, assume that Asians took full advantage of their forest environments, using perishable materials that leave no trace in the archaeological record. There was no need for specialized butchering tools, for hand-axes and cleavers. The different toolkits of Asia merely reflect entirely different environmental challenges.

Now Carl Swisher and Garniss Curtis of the Institute of Human Origins in Berkeley, working with Javanese paleoanthropologist Tenku Jacob, have produced new dates for *Homo erectus* in Java that suggest the movement out of Africa may have occurred considerably earlier. Curtis developed potassium-argon dating a quarter of a century ago. It was this technique for dating volcanic rocks that produced the then startling date of 1.75 million years ago for *Australopithecus boisei* at Olduvai Gorge in 1961.

28

As long ago as 1970 he applied a radioactive dating technique to volcanic pumice from fossil-bearing deposits at Mojokerto in central Java, where a fossil skull, estimated to be 1 million years old, had been found in 1936. To his surprise, Curtis acquired a reading closer to 2 million years ago from the Mojokerto deposits. His findings were suspect, however, for the kind of volcanic pumice at Mojokerto is difficult to date accurately. Twenty years later, Swisher and Curtis returned with a far more precise dating method than that from Curtis's earlier work on the Mojokerto pumice. They now date the Mojokerto skull to 1.8 million years ago and the Sangiran finds to 1.6 million, making them essentially the same date as the Lake Turkana finds in East Africa. The new dates have thrown the paleontological cat among the pigeons.

If there was a radiation of mammals, including humans, out of Africa about 2 million years ago, as the new dating implies, then humans spread across the Sahara into southeastern Asia with remarkable speed. Not that such rapid migration is an impossibility, for there is reason to believe the first Americans and Australians, despite their small numbers, raced across virgin continents during, or immediately after, the last Ice Age. *Homo erectus* may also have spread out of Africa before the hand-ax technology traditionally associated with them was fully developed, while our early ancestors were still using simple stone choppers and flakes. Thus, the tools of Southeast Asia may, in fact, reflect a much earlier technology, carried out of Africa and then adapted for the simple requirements of forest dwellers. Meanwhile, in the west new tools came into being as *Homo erectus* became more adept at hunting and butchering animals.

These scenarios are based on a mere handful of fossils scattered over an enormous area, and on stone-tool assemblages that are remarkable for telling us almost nothing about their users. Most experts still believe *Homo erectus* originated in Africa, and that earlier hominids like the Australopithecines and *Homo habilis* did not flourish in Asia. But the new dates tell us something about *Homo erectus* that has become increasingly clear about earlier and somewhat better-known hominids—they were far more varied in their development than one might think. Curtis and Swisher's new dates serve as a salutary reminder that we still know very little about *Homo erectus* and that many jolting surprises about the world 2 million years ago still await us. Therein lies the challenge of a search as complex and frustrating as that for the mythical snark. ☼

CHAPTER THREE
PREHISTORIC ARTISTS

Jean-Marie Chauvet has enthusiastically explored caves for more than 30 years, as a government caretaker with a passion for dark caves and the rock art found in them. "It is always the unknown that leads us," he says of the thousands of spelunkers who, like him, comb the gorges and dark caverns of Europe hoping for a fantastic discovery—best of all an undisturbed prehistoric art gallery. All of them know the story of France's Lascaux Cave, discovered in the dark, war-torn days of 1940 by some schoolboys out rabbit hunting with their dog. The dog disappeared into a rabbit hole and ended up in a buried cavern. The boys fetched a ladder and discovered a veritable Sistine Chapel of Cro-Magnon art dating to more than 15,000 years ago. Chauvet's spelunking grounds are the sheer cliffs and obscure defiles of the Ardèche Gorge in southern France. He knows every corner of the gorge, above and below ground, but realizes there are always new discoveries to be made. On Christmas Day, 1994, he and his friends were digging in an obscure chamber far underground, searching for a mysterious source of steady warm air. They opened a narrow hole, wriggled through, climbed a few feet along a narrow passage, and then dropped 30 feet by ladder onto a soft floor in what appeared to be a large chamber. Moments later, they shone their flashlights on the walls and were struck dumb with amazement. Perfectly preserved paintings of woolly rhinoceroses, bears, and other animals glistened around them. To their eternal credit, Chauvet and his colleagues retreated without disturbing anything and summoned leading experts on Cro-Magnon art. They had hit the spelunker's ultimate jackpot—a cave as magnificent as Altamira in northern Spain, or Lascaux itself. "As I studied them, I realized I was in the presence of the work of a great artist. It was like finding the work of an unknown Leonardo da Vinci," said Jean Clottes, France's leading authority on rock art. In prehistoric times, just as today, great artists were very rare.

What is now known as the Grotte de Chauvet was painted between 17,000 and 21,000 years ago, before a subterranean earth movement sealed the magnificent chambers. Long before humans penetrated the hillside, cave bears lived there in the dark. Chauvet and his colleagues have located the skeletons of at least 40 of these formidable beasts, many of their foot-long skulls visible just above the layers of calcite that have accumulated in their dens. The cave walls show fresh scratches where they sharpened their claws. A bear skull is perched in the center of one chamber, as if it were a prehistoric altar. French rock art expert Jean Clottes theorizes that the artists may have found the bear skeletons in the cave and considered the cave to be full of the bears' spirit. Thus, by painting bears and other dangerous animals, they would capture the spirit of the animals and imbue themselves with their power.

The Grotte de Chauvet, one of more than 300 painted caves in Europe, is unusual for its fine quality of paintings and for its depiction of more fearful animals, not only food quarry like bison, reindeer, and wild horses, which are common on other cave walls. For example, 40 woolly rhinoceros paintings appear on Chauvet's walls, more than twice the number depicted in other caves. The artists painted lions, bears, hyenas, and mammoths with carefully hatched lines depicting manes and body hair. Clearly, they were intimately familiar with their subjects and had a close relationship with them.

The discovery of the Grotte de Chauvet has caused a stir far outside the narrow coterie of prehistoric rock art specialists, for reasons that are not readily apparent. The painted chambers have been sealed off for as long as 15,000 years, meaning that the original context of the paintings is undisturbed. If the experts manage to uncover artifacts on the floors below the paintings, there is a chance that we may learn something about the activities that took place so deep in the earth. Herein lies the greatest fascination of this earliest of art traditions: why did the Cro-Magnons choose to decorate cave walls? Was it art for art's sake, created for sheer enjoyment? Even the earliest investigators rejected this theory, on the grounds that prehistoric peoples lived much closer to the animal world. They believed the art was a form of what they called "sympathetic hunting magic," a form of pictorial spell designed to make animals easier to hunt. In recent years, the computer has come into play as an analytical tool. Rock art specialists have used them

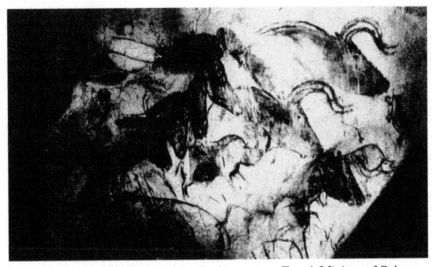

Grotte de Chauvet: wild bulls and woolly rhinoceroses. French Ministry of Culture. Reprinted with permission.

to study the distributions of different animals on cave walls, attempting to unravel the complicated palimpsests of figures in different friezes. French scholar André Leroi-Gourhan argued that the art was not random, but rather part of a system of meanings that formed the world view of the artists. For example, by counting the associations of subjects and clusters of motifs, Leroi-Gourhan found that certain themes, among them female figures, appear in rock shelters and better locales, whereas others were in dark caverns. Yet, like everyone else, he was unable to decipher their meaning.

We know that many hunter-gatherer groups use ritual and art, creating and manipulating visual forms to structure their existence and give meaning to it. Anthropologists working among diverse peoples have shown how many artistic traditions use artistic principles like symmetry that underlie every aspect of life, from social relationships to village planning. People may use even comparatively few symbols and their carefully defined contexts to communicate important meanings. The Cro-Magnons obviously thought in terms of continuities between animal and human life, and with their own social world. Thus, their art was a symbolic depiction of these continuities. The artist selected a specific animal to paint or engrave, and a certain wall area to use not just because he or she liked it, but because of the symbolic meanings involved. Some archaeologists believe that the underground art, with its accurate depictions of reindeer and other animals at different times of year, may have been a kind of storehouse of knowledge about the environment, passed down from one generation to the next, in a society where life spans were short and all information was communicated orally, often within a context of shamanistic ritual, chant, and dance.

The world of the Cro-Magnons was totally different from our own. We are separated from it by some 15,000 years of dramatic climatic and environmental change, by a chasm of years that we can never bridge effectively enough to understand their intricate religious beliefs. Just how complicated these beliefs were can be discerned by looking at San art in southern Africa. The ancestry of the San hunter-gatherers of South Africa goes back more than 10,000 years, to the late Ice Age and even earlier. The ancestors of the modern-day San, who survive only in a few arid enclaves like the Kalahari Desert, may be the primordial inhabitants of southern Africa, direct descendants of the first modern humans. They are known to us from their diminutive, simple artifacts, and from a magnificent treasury of rock art found on the walls of caves and rockshelters in such areas as South Africa's Drakensberg Mountains. San art is very different from that of the Cro-Magnons. The artists drew running hunters, people fishing from boats and gathering honey, camp scenes, and dances. The hunters can be seen stalking game in disguise, hotly pursuing wounded quarry, even raiding the cattle herds of their agricultural neighbors. For years, archaeologists have used San paintings as an archive of information on late prehistoric lifeways. But South African archaeologist David Lewis-Williams has shown that many of the paintings depict complex metaphors that represent symbolic values in the San world. He discovered long-forgotten San oral traditions collected by Victorian anthropologist and linguist Wilhelm Bleek. Bleek's informants recounted some of the chants and rituals behind the paintings. Each association of human figures and animals, it seemed, had profound meaning to the artists and the people.

Many Drakensberg scenes depict eland with dancers cavorting around them. Lewis-Williams has used oral traditions to decipher some of these scenes. The elongated bodies of the dancers convey a sense of being stretched out that is felt by people in an altered state of consciousness. In deep trance, the dancers feel a boiling sensation as supernatural power passes

34

up their spines. Some San groups considered themselves the "people of the eland." The eland is rich in meat and vital byproducts that can sustain families for weeks. San myths associate the eland with sweet-smelling honey, a similar scent to that which emanates from a dead eland when it is skinned. A San shaman will dance alongside the carcass of a freshly killed eland. He enters a trance and cures everyone of ills by removing the "arrows of sickness" that may be directed against them. At one Drakensberg rockshelter, Lewis-Williams found a painting of an eland in its death throes. Dancers cavort around the animal, one adorned with cloven antelope hoofs, crossed like those of the dying beast. White dots depict sweat drops falling from a dancer "dying" in trance. He believes the dancers are acquiring the potency released by the death of the eland, their trances being so powerful that they become like eland themselves. The being of the shaman and the people becomes merged with that of the most potent of all animals.

The eland was by no means the only animal with a close relationship to the artist. Every San painting, every frieze, every superposition, depicted a network of relationships that held profound meaning for the artists and the shamans who looked after the well-being of the group. But can we interpret the Chauvet paintings in similar terms? We know that San artists and their ancestors have been at work since the late Ice Age; indeed, they may have been painting at the same time as the Cro-Magnons. But it would be rash to take the symbolic relationships of a century ago and transfer them over a chasm of 15,000 years. After generations of admiring and studying the earliest of art traditions, we must admit we will likely never fathom the deepest meanings of the symbolism behind the Chauvet paintings or their relatives from other European caves. Yet we can be sure that the artists were concerned not solely with pure artistry but more with communicating vitally important and intensely symbolic messages that passed the knowledge and experience of one generation to the next, explaining the often frightening and violent world around them. The paintings fill us with respect for their brilliant artistry, which, perhaps, we appreciate even more than its original artists did. But they also fill us with awe and admiration for the complex and sophisticated hunter-gatherer societies that flourished in environments far more demanding than our own. 🌑

CHAPTER FOUR

REFLECTIONS ON
THE KAFUE FLATS

I will never forget Zambia's Kafue Flats. It was there, many years ago, that I realized there was more to archaeology than just scientific methods. Few people outside Zambia have heard of the Flats—a vast, seasonally inundated floodplain where the altitude varies by but a few feet across more than a hundred miles. In April, the meandering Kafue River spills over its banks and floods the treeless, featureless alluvium. The waters recede slowly during the dry season. Swamp-loving lechwe antelope and zebra still feed on the short grass at flood's edge, just as they have done for thousands of years.

We had been digging a well-preserved 3,500-year-old Stone Age hunting camp at the Gwisho hot springs on the edge of the Flats. The excavations were a great success. The trenches yielded not only stone artifacts but a wealth of animal bones and vegetable remains, unusual in a site of this age.

The Gwisho hot springs must have been an ideal place for Stone Age hunters. These hot springs bubble up on the margins of the ubiquitous savanna woodland, creating an oasis of bubbling water and green, reedy swamps. It was easy to imagine the primeval landscape, the patchwork of dry woodland, lush swamp, and grassy flats, probably little changed from today. But there were few animals to be seen. The occasional duiker and zebra appeared on the horizon; guinea fowl strutted close to the site. But there were none of the dense herds reported by Victorian explorers and sportsmen on the banks of the Kafue.

That day 27 years ago, I had been counting broken lechwe and warthog teeth by the dozen, quantifying faunal statistics in dizzying profusion. It was all very impersonal—just bone counts and some scanty impressions of young and mature animals, hunted with wood-tipped poisoned arrows, found in the excavations. Come evening, I was weary of bones and quartz artifacts. The shadows from the westering sun cast a yellow light over the Flats. The shallow waters shimmered in the evening sun. A herd of lechwe fed by the water's edge.

As I sat and watched the feeding herd in the sunset, the artifacts and bones of Gwisho came to life. I felt like an ancient hunter, lying in the grass, watching for lone strays, studying the intricate movements of the unsuspecting antelope. For that magic hour, I watched a prehistoric landscape, the eternal cycle of game feeding and settling down for the night. It was as if the lechwe had never heard a rifle or competed with domestic herds for grazing space. The gathering dusk finally snapped me back to the present. But for days afterward, I felt like the prophet Ezekiel in the valley of bones that came to life with flesh and blood. Just for a moment, I had peered into a vanished, remote world—a world far removed from ours.

I have made other momentary visits to that world: camping in wild country by the banks of the Zambezi River, sleeping in the open and hearing lions roar at the moon; walking through thick bush near the Luangwa River in eastern Zambia, close to a herd of feeding elephants. The giant creatures moved surprisingly quietly, their stomachs growling softly in the late afternoon heat. I remember wondering how a Stone Age hunter with a wooden spear would have killed such beasts. I still treasure those rare moments when prehistory lingered in the air, elusive, evocative, and remote.

In a generation or so, few people will be able to see Africa wearing even a fraction of its prehistoric clothing. Except for the big game in a handful of parks, the African fauna will have gone the way of megafauna everywhere—into extinction. With the animals will vanish a vast repository of hunting lore and tracking skill that still lingers in parts of Africa to this day. Despite highly sophisticated studies of African hunter-gatherers and many anthropological studies of subsistence farmers, surprisingly little attention has been paid to the nuts and bolts of traditional African hunting methods and tracking skills. How did Stone Age hunters kill elephants? What were prehistoric success rates? What strategies did hunters use to pursue wary impala antelope and lumbering buffalo? To answer such questions requires months of arduous participatory observation during the hunt—and few anthropologists have done this.

One shining exception is the American Stuart Marks, who in the mid-1960s spent ten months studying the hunting methods of the Luangwa Valley Bisa, hunters and farmers in a remote part of eastern Zambia. There hunters used inaccurate muzzle-loading muskets just like those carried by Napoleon's soldiers. So they had to rely on hunting and stalking skills like those developed millennia before, in the Stone Age. The Bisa thought of themselves as predators, like lions and hyenas. "I also belong to the chase," proclaims one of their proverbs. Their success depended not on twentieth-century technology, but on prehistoric expertise.

Over many months Marks became familiar with the local game populations, and with the routes and hunting patterns followed by individual hunters. He accompanied Bisa hunters on dozens of hunts—after buffalo, elephant, hippopotamus, warthog, and antelope large and small. He talked to old men who remembered the ancient elephant-hunting guilds and their methods. A group of hunters would slip in among an elephant herd. The leader would wound one of the great animals. Then the other hunters moved in with weighted spears along its escape route. There were other, less direct methods, too. Sometimes experienced hunters would climb trees and cast spears at elephants passing underneath, aiming for a vulnerable point between the shoulder blades. Many times, the hunters would dig large pits along game paths and line the bottoms with sharp spears. The elephant would crash through the grass and pole covering and could be speared at leisure.

Bisa hunters were especially skilled at stalking buffalo. The stalker would commit himself to a specific herd long before the stalk began. Large herds leave abundant traces of their passing. The hunters claimed they could tell how long ago a herd had passed simply by examining fresh droppings. They would then test the wind direction, study the composition of the herd, and begin the stalk. Marks watched them approach their prey, moving forward as the animals faced the other way or were feeding, freezing when they looked up and stared. Once in position, the hunter fired his ancient musket. Seven out of ten times he missed. And if a hit was scored, the animal was almost never killed outright. As in Stone Age times, it could be hours, even days, before the hunter could catch up with his quarry and kill it, having tracked the beast over many miles. In many cases, the wounded animal escaped or was killed and eaten by lions before the hunter arrived.

For centuries the Bisa lived in their remote homeland. They used simple hunting methods that provided an adequate meat supply, yet they never depleted game stocks to dangerous levels. In a sense, Marks lived prehistory, for the Bisa farmers still presumably use the same basic stalking and trapping methods as the Stone Age hunter-gatherers who had dwelt in the Luangwa Valley before them. I am sure that there were moments when Marks, like me, felt a close affinity to a vanished past, a time when humans lived by hunting alone. What counted more than anything else was not technology, but an intimate knowledge of the animals' habits and of the natural environment.

In these days of all-out science and hi-tech archaeology: it is distinctly unfashionable to talk of emotional reactions to the past. But find me a serious archaeologist who does not experience moments of intuitive reve-lation, a sense of walking among the prehistoric people. It is this quality of intuition, of imagination, that makes archaeology unique among the social sciences. We are fortunate in Africa to have some last remnants of the prehistoric world to help us understand an increasingly remote past.

As I watched the Kafue lechwe, back in 1961, I remembered Frederick Courtney Selous, who was the epitome of the 1880s Victorian hunter—he had decimated Africa's game. Oddly enough, we had—at quite different times, of course—both attended the same school. Selous's sharp-eyed, bearded countenance stared down at us from the walls of the school hall. I always felt slightly intimidated by his stare, and suspected he hung there to remind us to serve God, country, and Empire. That evening on the Kafue I suddenly realized that this imposing figure had, at times, been little more than a butcher. He, and his even more indiscriminate contemporaries, wiped out more African game in a generation than did millions of years of prehistoric hunting.

I was interested enough to look up what Selous had written about the lechwe antelope. Well, he admired their graceful antics: "When pursued they usually take to the water, dashing through the shallow lagoons . . . with a series of plunges, each spring being taken from the bottom, even when the water is almost up to their necks." But Selous was ever the sportsman. "The elegant lyrate horns of the males are among the handsomest of the trophies to be won," he wrote. So to him the lechwe were just meat and trophies on the hoof. Selous's collection of trophy heads now molders in museums and on the walls of trendy boutiques frequented by interior designers. Thanks to Victorian rifles, the Kafue Flats is one of the very few places where you can still see lechwe leaping and plunging in the wild. In all fairness to Selous, it should be emphasized that, in time, he was one of those responsible for the development of modern views on wildlife conservation and management.

While Selous and his contemporaries were astute observers of game, they took no more than a passing interest in the anonymous retainers who served as their trackers and guides. In a bitter irony of history, these quiet local people applied the skills of centuries and millennia to provide target practice for their masters. But the "sportsmen" used not bows and arrows but repeater rifles, and dangerously depleted the game population.

Thinking about Selous and the Kafue after all these years prompts another thought. Are we not doing the same ourselves to the archaeological record? Pot hunters and looters are wiping out thousands of archaeological sites a year, often using hi-tech site-location methods developed by the archaeologists who are their enemies. I suspect that sometime in the twenty-first century our successors may label us as the anonymous guides who helped others destroy the past.

But the future may not be so bleak. Archaeologists have new and sophisticated weapons for fleshing out prehistoric lifeways—increasingly fine-grained data recovery and analytical methods. Major theoretical advances and occasional remarkable insights into prehistory from studies of living societies are at their disposal. With ingenuity, motivation, and curiosity, we can achieve a remarkably complete picture of the past. Our archaeological descendants may respect us for trying to do our best under almost impossible circumstances. ❀

CHAPTER FIVE
PRECOCIOUS FISHERFOLK

How many archaeologists have heard of the Jomon? Relatively few, I wager, for Japanese prehistory is hardly a mainstream specialty in American archaeological circles. More's the pity, for the Jomon people, whose culture flourished from ca 10,000 to 300 B.C., made some of the earliest pottery in the world. Not the earliest—that honor presently goes to the inhabitants of the Fukui and Kamikuroiwa Caves in southwestern Japan, whose appliqué and fingernail decorated potsherds have been radio-carbon dated to about 10,000 B.C. At first, Japanese archaeologists disbelieved these dates, assuming, like everyone else, that farmers were the first people to manufacture and use clay vessels.

Many years ago my Cambridge University supervisor pounced on an essay of mine in which I had failed to mention pottery in the same breath as an early farming settlement in Egypt's Fayum, a once fertile lake depression west of the Nile River. "Pottery—farmers make that," he told me with dogmatic finality. In those halcyon days Vere Gordon Childe straddled archaeology like a colossus. His concept of a "Neolithic Revolution" provided a definitive link between ceramics and farming. Only a year later, however, Kathleen Kenyon discovered "Pre-pottery Neolithic" levels at Jericho, and Childe's theoretical edifice crumbled around our heads. We soon learned the ancient world was far more complicated than anyone had ever imagined. Some village dwellers had the temerity to farm before they made pottery, while others, such as Japan's Jomon people, were potters long before they cultivated the land. There were, in fact, people throughout much of East Asia who established permanent settlements in areas rich in predictable food supplies, and who adopted the art of pottery before agriculture.

The word Jomon means "cord-marked," an apt description of their pottery, the surface of which was so decorated. To date, some 254 different types of Jomon pottery have been identified, each with its own chronological and spatial distribution—a nightmare of archaeological complexity even for the most ardent classifier.

The earliest surviving Jomon vessels, manufactured before 9000 B.C., are simple cooking pots with pointed bases. Over the years Jomon artisans developed much more complicated shapes including elaborate bottles and pedestaled bowls. By 3000 B.C., some communities manufactured pots with elaborately sculptured rims, now, unfortunately, a favorite of collectors of ancient Asian art. We know that Jomon potters were masters of their craft, but if they weren't practicing agriculture, what enabled them to thrive in permanent settlements and allowed them the leisure necessary to make pots?

Asia in 10,000 B.C. was quite different from today. Siberia was joined to Alaska and the Great Yellow Plain linked the Korean Peninsula and mainland China. Only narrow ocean passages separated Hokkaido and Honshu from Korea. By 6000 B.C., the shorelines of the Japanese islands and Korean Peninsula were close to their modern configurations, the Great Yellow Plain had become the Yellow Sea, and dozens of large Ice Age mammals had become extinct with global warming. The Japanese of the day responded by living off smaller game, more plant foods, and the abundant and varied sea creatures. Some groups were so successful they established permanent villages, where enormous piles of discarded mollusk shells accumulated over time.

Shell middens are invaluable to archaeologists for the archives of many coastal groups are writ large in these dullest of all site features. The well-preserved Jomon middens provide a rather complete occupational history of nearby villages. In some instances the same location was inhabited for generations, either permanently or on a seasonal basis. In the Kanto region of southeastern Honshu, great circular shell middens surround groups of 30 to 2,000 pit-houses. At other sites the houses are clustered around a central plaza.

Like pottery, permanent residence at a site is interpreted as an indicator of a higher level of social complexity than that enjoyed by small nomadic family bands. As so often happens in archaeology, claiming a site was occupied year round is one thing, establishing it in the archaeological record is another. In the case of the Jomon, Japanese archaeologists have turned to the esoteric but revealing study of annual growth rings in clam shells. They have shown how many villages enjoyed a peak shellfish collecting season in the spring, while others did most of their foraging in summer or winter. However, most larger villages show a pattern of low-level collecting throughout the year, as if their inhabitants took at least some shellfish every month, while devoting most of their attention to other seasonal foods.

Jomon communities lived along a coastline with numerous snug bays and shallow inlets, estuaries and rocky outcrops, where the distribution of food resources varied greatly from one mile to the next. And while only a few Jomon sites have yielded the kind of comprehensive subsistence data that is so common from North American and European settlements, Japanese scholars have been able to piece together a cultural picture by combining data from numerous sites. In the spring, the Jomon collected shellfish and sprouting edible plants, in summer they turned to fishing and the hunting of sea mammals. By late summer, they scoured shellfish beds, drying the meat for winter. In the fall they harvested nuts, which provided high-protein food during the lean, cold months. Even in the depth of winter they continued to hunt sea mammals as well as deer and wild boar. Everything depended on intensive exploitation of different animal and plant foods as they came into season, and on the processing and storage of large quantities of dried seafood and nuts. A combination of the two enabled many Jomon communities to remain at the same location for long periods of time.

I am irresistibly reminded of coastal hunter-gatherer societies of the Americas, particularly the Chumash people of southern California, who relied heavily on fishing, the hunting of sea mammals, and on fall acorn harvests. Many Chumash groups settled in large, permanent communities governed by powerful chiefs and traded with neighboring groups over a wide area. In the Midwest, communities flourished in densely populated river valleys rich in fish and plants, as witnessed by Stuart Streuver's excavations at Koster in the Illinois Valley. And, in southeast Alaska and the Pacific Northwest, hunter-gatherer societies sustained themselves with salmon and other fish, which they dried and stored. However, as Herbert Maschner has shown in his recent excavations at Tebenkof Bay, Alaska, the ability to preserve food fluctuated considerably over the centuries, partly because of changes in available resources.

The Jomon were skilled fisherfolk who took at least 50 species of river, coastal, and deep-water fish, as well as dolphin, the oil from which still adheres to some Jomon pot walls. From the earliest times they used bone fishhooks and within several millennia they were bringing down sea mammals with toggle-headed harpoons, so effective in the Bering Strait region. Jomon fishermen were expert seafarers, apparently venturing quite far offshore. Though we know of no planked boats like those used by the Chumash, the remains of several dugout canoes have been recovered from their middens.

What are we to make of these remarkable fisherfolk—Noble Savages, living in a land of bountiful seafood and predictable plenty? There is something very captivating about the image of people who never starved and never had to work for their food, while living in permanent villages in sheltered, sun-dappled bays. However, as biological anthropologists Patricia Lambert and Phil Walker have demonstrated, this stereotype is grossly misleading. Bones of the ancient Chumash show clear signs of dietary stress, malnutrition, and epidemic disease brought about by people living in close proximity to one another. Lambert has also studied the incidence of warfare through bone traumas. There are many more casualties in Chumash cemeteries in later centuries, suggesting an increase in warfare, perhaps in response to rising populations and competition for food resources.

As far as the Chumash are concerned, one problem was the El Niño, the celebrated atmospheric change that periodically brings storms and warmer currents to California shores, virtually wiping out coastal fishing. Another factor was the sheer unpredictability of the local climate. The Chumash responded by exchanging foodstuffs with kin living in other environments, spreading the risk , as it were, so the effects of food shortage were minimized. But, inevitably, they sometimes went hungry.

The homeland of the Jomon, with its potential for permanent settlement, may also seem like paradise on Earth, but I suspect each community faced the same general problems as the Chumash—rising populations, periodic food shortages, and dramatic differences in food supply from one region to the next. Some areas like Tokyo Bay were indeed rich in aquatic and plant foods, but other coastlines had relatively little to offer. Thanks to their encyclopedic knowledge of Jomon pots, Japanese archaeologists have been able to plot the changing distributions of Tokyo Bay village sites, which follow rising and falling sea levels over the millennia. But even as coastlines receded, some communities stayed inland and turned from exploiting marine mollusks to varieties found in nearby rivers, as if there was competition for coastal shellfish beds. Most likely, the Jomon people responded to growing population densities and to dietary stress in exactly the same way as the Chumash—by trading foodstuffs with neighbors, by improving food storage, and by intensifying the food quest. Or, like the Koster people of the American Midwest, they began to take up agriculture to supplement the food supply. However humble the crops were—barnyard grass and millet—the transition toward agriculture began long before rice and other major cultigens entered Japan from the mainland. By 5700 B.C., some western Japanese communities may have cleared forest for cultivation on a large scale.

Although the Jomon people are to be admired for their ceramic virtuosity, they were among the most sophisticated and expert hunters and foragers in the prehistoric world. ☀

CHAPTER SIX
TAMING THE AUROCHS

Behold *Bos primigenius*, a large formidable animal with curving horns and irascible personality. He is the primordial wild ox, or aurochs, prancing across the walls of France's Lascaux cave, the Sistine Chapel of Cro-Magnon art. Even though the beasts had been domesticated for some 6,000 years by Roman times, Julius Caesar, upon seeing wild aurochs in Gaul in 56 B.C., remarked that "even if they are caught very young, the animals cannot be tamed or accustomed to human beings." Although the last known herd of wild aurochs perished in the forests of Poland in the early seventeenth century, Polish scientists did manage to "back breed" a herd just before the Second World War, producing a frisky, russet-colored animal of uncertain temper, not unlike its ferocious predecessor. How did our prehistoric forebears manage to tame such an unpredictable, solitary animal eight millennia ago? Something had to have happened to both man and animal to make the domestication of *Bos primigenius* possible.

In the 1930s, that learned but eccentric archaeologist Vere Gordon Childe used the term "Neolithic Revolution" to describe the cultural transformation in which humans abandoned their hunter-gatherer ways in favor of farming and animal husbandry. Childe believed this revolution began in the Near East at the end of the Ice Age when much drier conditions prevailed; humans and animals were brought into closer contact as they sought and used the same oases. According to Childe, hunter-gatherers were soon penning young animals and maintaining them as an assured meat supply. These events ultimately led to the animals' domestication.

Childe's oasis theory was so appealing that it became part of Arnold Toynbee's *History of the World* (1934–1954), and still appears in many reference books to this day. However, as archaeologists have long known, it is far too simplistic. After all, wild animals do not change their habits overnight and settle down close to their predators, nor do hunters suddenly embrace their prey when the climate turns drier.

Many years ago, I was looking for early farming villages along the banks of the Zambezi River when I wandered inadvertently into the midst of a peaceful herd of feeding elephants. I was new to the bush and not familiar with the tell-tale signs of their presence—snapped-off branches, fresh dung, and the gentle burblings emanating from their bellies. Upon seeing them, I froze. They looked at me nonchalantly and then resumed snacking. I quietly retraced my steps and left them in peace. They were not alarmed by my presence since I was in full view and moving slowly, posing no threat. Herein may lie a clue to the taming of *Bos primigenius*.

Biologist Michael Mloszewski has spent months observing herds of wild buffalo (*Synceros caffer*) in central Africa. Wild buffalo roam in well-watered woodland and grassland habitats as well as in much drier environments, where regular movement between pasture and permanent water sources is the key to survival. The largest herds congregate in better watered environments. Animals in drier environments travel in smaller and more docile groups, reflecting a need to stay with the herd in its meandering search for water.

Mloszewski not only watched the herds, he walked among them, just as I had done with the Zambezi elephants. He found the buffalo wary of carnivores and other possible threats hidden by the trees or tall grass. The herd was more relaxed when a potential predator was out in the open, walking slowly among them. Presumably, prehistoric game herds, even those of *Bos primigenius*, by all accounts as unpredictable an animal as the ill-tempered buffalo, may have acted in the same way, allowing hunters to move among them provided they were in sight. Such free movement was vital to people who had but the simplest of hunting technologies such as the spear or bow, for they could come close to their prey without arousing too much suspicion.

Archaeologist Andrew Smith of the University of Cape Town, South Africa, has studied pastoralist groups in, and on the fringes of, the Sahara. The desert was much smaller as recently as 6500 B.C. Semi-arid grassland and shallow freshwater lakes covered much of what are now arid plains. Antelope of all kinds abounded in this landscape, as did *Bos primigenius*. A small and scattered population of hunters, fishers, and foragers also flourished in the desert, living close to permanent water supplies. Then, about 6000 B.C., climatic conditions over North Africa and the Near East changed. The desert expanded, springs and streams dried up, and grasslands withered. These were the conditions, Smith believes, that led to the domestication of wild cattle.

Even before the drought, the Sahara was never well-watered. Both humans and animals were constantly on the move, in search of food and reliable water supplies. Under these circumstances, Smith believes, the small herds of *Bos primigenius* became even smaller, closer knit breeding units. The beasts were better behaved, making it easier for hunters to move among them, predict their habits, and cull them at will. It was under these conditions that cattle and humans came into close contact—exactly as Childe had suggested a half century ago.

But contrary to Childe's model, this symbiosis did not lead to domestication. Smith believes that the hunters were well aware of the ways in which their prey behaved. At first, they controlled the movement of the herd, preventing it from moving from one place to another, thus assuring continuance of their meat supply. By culling the more intemperate animals, they soon gained genetic control over the beasts, which led to rapid physiological changes in the herd. The newly domesticated animals were easier to control and may have enjoyed a higher calving rate, which would have yielded greater milk supplies. Judging by rock paintings deep in the Sahara, herders were soon selecting for hide color and horn shape.

Andrew Smith's hypothesis was developed for the Sahara region, but it is still unclear whether domesticated cattle were tamed independently in North Africa, or introduced into the continent from the Near East. It seems entirely likely that much of the same process of control occurred in both the Near East and in North Africa, among peoples who had an intimate knowledge of wild cattle behavior. Living in ever drier environments, they cast around for alternative, more predictable food supplies. Within 2,000 years of the first domestication, cattle herders had spread throughout the Near East, deep into Asia, to the far frontiers of Western Europe, and as far south as the East African highlands—with drastic consequences for the global environment. Experts suspect, for example, that chronic overgrazing helped to destroy Saharan vegetation, already withered by drought, as early as 4000 B.C.

If Andrew Smith is correct, it was a combination of drought, profound familiarity with prey, and, as always, brilliant human opportunism that domesticated one of the Ice Age's most intractable, curmudgeonly beasts. ❀

CHAPTER SEVEN
NEOLITHIC NEWGRANGE

Ancient Irish legends call Newgrange the Abode of Oengus, son of Dagda, the pre-Celtic god of the Sun. Archaeologists know it as one of the finest megalithic passage-graves in Europe. Located in Ireland's Boyne Valley some 30 miles north of Dublin, Newgrange lies at the heart of a great concentration of Neolithic burial mounds. Ever since the site was discovered in 1699, people have wondered who built it and why. Native Irish, the Romans, and even the Phoenicians were cited until archaeologist Michael O'Kelly of University College, Cork, painstakingly excavated the great mound between 1962 and 1975. His excavation and survey work, along with restoration and stabilization of the mound, revealed that it was built ca. 3150 B.C. by Stone Age farmers who raised cattle and cultivated barley much as Irish farmers did until a century ago.

Some 280 feet in diameter, the giant mound stands atop a low ridge about three-quarters of a mile north of the Boyne River. Faced in gleaming white quartz, it is visible for miles even on an overcast day. I visited Newgrange on such a day. Clare Tuffy, the site's manager, showed me around.

Four standing stones are all that remain of a large stone circle that once surrounded the grave. The core of the mound is built of large water-worn boulders and layers of stabilizing turf. Large slabs of stone incised with enigmatic spiral and zigzag patterns surround its base.

We walked through a 62-foot-long narrow passageway that leads to a single burial chamber, an oval room 17 feet long. Three recesses off the chamber give it a cruciform shape. The ceiling of the passage is six feet high and made of large slabs or overlapping boulders that form a corbel vault. The roof in the central chamber is 20 feet high and is made of boulders tightly packed with clay and sand. O'Kelly found cleverly placed grooves pecked into boulders designed to carry rainwater away from the apex of the

Newgrange, Boyne Valley, Ireland. Courtesy Department of Public Works, Government of Ireland. Reprinted with permission.

chamber, effectively keeping it dry for 5,000 years. Each recess contains a basin stone, where the bones of the dead were deposited. Remains from at least four people were recovered, two of whom had been cremated. These finds may represent only a fraction of the original deposits, since the tomb has been open to visitors, souvenir hunters among them, for nearly 300 years.

When O'Kelly excavated the mound's entrance, he uncovered what he called a "roof box," a niche built just above the door lintel. He speculated that the niche had served as a container for offerings to the dead, but was puzzled by a three-foot-long rectangular slit cut into its floor. Newgrange's entrance faces southeast. Local legends spoke of sunlight penetrating through to the main chamber on the winter solstice. On December 21, 1969, O'Kelly and a team of observers watched as the upper edge of the sun appeared above the eastern horizon beyond the Boyne River. At 8:58 A.M., he reported "the first pencil of direct sunlight shone through the roof box and along the passage to reach across the tomb as far as the front edge of the basin stone in the end recess." The mystery of the slit was solved. Today, visitors who gather at the site on the winter solstice must wait four and one-half minutes after sunrise to witness the event because the position of earth's axis relative to the sun has precessed westward over the years. There is no shortage of applicants for this special visit. The chamber can accommodate only 20 people and there is a ten-year waiting list for a December 21 visit. Luckily for visitors, the effect of the sun shining through the passage on the winter solstice is re-created daily with lights.

From Newgrange I traveled to nearby Knowth, another famous passage-grave somewhat more complex than Newgrange. Knowth has two entrances, one on the east and one on the west, aligned with the summer solstice. Each passage leads to a separate burial chamber. George Eogan of University College, Dublin, is excavating and restoring the collapsed eastern passage, the first stage of a conservation effort. According to Eogan, this 5,000-year-old mound was built atop the remains of an older farming settlement dating to 4000 B.C. The mound was reused as an Iron Age fort between 300 B.C. and A.D. 600, a Christian settlement from the eighth to tenth centuries A.D., and a Norman stronghold in the twelfth century.

While poring over the spirals and checkerboard patterns on the weathered rocks, I wondered about the significance of these imposing megaliths. My guess is that Newgrange and Knowth were the resting places of revered ancestors, or guardians of the lands in which their sepulchers lay. They were also places where people gathered to observe the passage of the seasons, the cycles of life and death, of fertility, birth, growth, and harvest. ✺

CHAPTER EIGHT
NEW FINDS AT FLAG FEN

Long-term excavations are few and far between in these days of budgetary restraint and widespread salvage archaeology. Flag Fen is one of the exceptions, for Francis Pryor and Maisie Taylor are devoting the better part of a lifetime to this most complicated and intriguing of archaeological sites. Flag Fen lies on the edges of the eastern English fens, a mysterious, waterlogged platform of collapsed wooden structures, walkways, and a post alignment connecting the site to higher ground, dating to about 1350 B.C. For centuries, the local farmers cast offerings of valuable metal tools—and sometimes human bones—into the dark waters of the fen. Pryor and Taylor believe the site was connected to an extensive Bronze Age field system at nearby Fengate, although the significance of the platform and long, irregular post alignment still eludes them. Was Flag Fen an important ritual center, where people cast offerings into shallow water in symbolic offerings to the forces of the spiritual world? Or did the site have a more prosaic function, perhaps as a cattle enclosure set in the midst of the waters for protection? On a recent visit to England, I was able to spend a day at Flag Fen and obtain an update on this most fascinating of archaeological sites anywhere.

Flag Fen was much transformed from my last visit two years ago, but just as puzzling as ever. Pryor and Taylor have completed the excavation of the original main trench in the heart of the site, exposing part of the artificial platform to near-bedrock. They now believe they have found walkways extending across the humanly-made island, narrow pathways laid between posts, with occasional gaps in the edges to allow access, perhaps by boat, or from other paths. There are intriguing traces, too, of a walkway that stretches toward the higher ground at Fengate to the west. More walkways have appeared in a new excavation on the eastern side of the Mustdyke, the Fenland channel that bisects Flag Fen. Thanks to the generosity of local companies, a permanent wooden exhibition hall covers the newly excavated trench where you can see no fewer than four walkways dating from 900 to 1300 B.C. The narrow tracks are again delineated by often substantial posts, and appear to be covered with a thin layer of gravel. They are narrow enough for pedestrians laden with food or supplies, but not for carts, which were probably too wide, and perhaps too heavy, to pass across the wetlands. It is still too early to say where these walkways, or those on the platform, lead, but it is a reasonable guess they led to the higher ground of Northey Island to the east. Here, Pryor has made another new and important discovery.

A dry and warm summer in 1994 dried out the local farmland so much that it provided an unusual opportunity for detailed aerial photography at a revealing scale impossible for many years. The new pictures have revealed at least 60 acres of an intact Bronze Age field system, including both field boundaries and small, undisturbed burial mounds on the better-drained land of Northey Island on the eastern side of the platform and opposite Fengate. Francis Pryor is deeply intrigued by the opportunity to explore this well-preserved field system, where preservation may be exceptional, especially in the lower, less well drained levels. If he is right about preservation conditions, this may be the only field system in Britain to yield organic materials on a large scale. If all goes well, he hopes to excavate a sample of the field system in the next couple of years.

I was lucky enough to visit the new Flag Fen Visitor Center while the latest spectacular discovery was still on display. During the 1994 excavations, a large part of a wooden plank wheel came to light, at 1100 B.C. the earliest of its kind yet discovered in Britain. The alder wheel fragment is in near-perfect condition, with two oak braces still in position, binding together the thick planks. Over a third of the wheel has survived, so beautifully preserved that the worn edge, complete with gravel embedded in the wood, can be clearly discerned. One of the oak dowels joining (as opposed to bracing) the wheels still lies in its carefully drilled hole. While there is nothing unusual about the design of the plank wheel, already known from later contexts, the weathered edge with its gravel gives the find an immediacy rare among artifacts of any kind. English Heritage is currently conserving the wheel by freeze-drying it. Eventually, it will go on permanent display at the Visitor Center.

Flag Fen continues to yield remarkable artifacts, the most important being two well-preserved fragments of an Iron Age short sword scabbard, found between two posts in July 1993, and dating to roughly the second to fifth centuries B.C. The copper alloy front plate is 450 mm long, 55 mm wide at the widest point, and only 1 mm thick. Incised lines adorn the front plate, with spiral-like circles at the top, perhaps a schematic rendering of a Celtic "dragon-pair" motif found on an Iron Age dagger of 300 B.C. from Hungary. Pryor compares the front plate to a scabbard of the first to second centuries B.C. found at Hunsbury in southern England. Like other ceremonial offerings at Flag Fen, the scabbard was deliberately broken before being thrown away. The find is important in itself, but in addition offers testimony to the durability of traditional religious rituals, which survived at Flag Fen from at least 1300 B.C. to the very threshold of Roman times a thousand years later. It is remarkable that so much of Britain's prehistoric metalwork comes from lakes and streams, highlighting the great importance of water in Celtic and earlier rituals.

Today's archaeology requires very fine-grained excavation techniques and the cooperation of scientists from many disciplines. By the same token, excellent preservation conditions are all-important, especially if we are to grapple with thorny questions like the nature of ancient religious beliefs, as well as minor details of prehistoric subsistence and farming practices. This is what makes Flag Fen such a unique laboratory of cutting-edge archaeological research, much of it carried out within a carefully defined environmental context. The remarkably complete environmental data allows the archaeologists to build convincing replicas not merely of houses, but of the associated field systems as well. Pryor and Taylor have reconstructed parts of a Bronze Age field system complete with droveways, houses, and reconstituted livestock, which provide visitors (and archaeologists, for that matter) with a lively appreciation of what the ancient landscape looked like and how the people may have adjusted to its realities. For example, I never knew that the thatched roof of a prehistoric hut would rot in damp climates if the house was not kept warm with a hearth. And during my visit, I helped feed the fat Flag Fen pigs, animals as close to their Bronze Age ancestors as modern breeding can get. Such experiences make one realize just how important these animals were to ancient European farmers. But what makes Flag Fen unique is its remarkable archaeological jigsaw puzzle represented by its myriad planks, posts, and timbers. You can see how the ancient woodworkers recycled seasoned oak uprights from their houses and pens for the edges of the walkways: given new use, tenon holes and all. And the same timbers lie in the excavation at your feet. Flag Fen offers a remarkable archaeological record, but beyond that also a testimony to just how little we know about the past, with our rows of stones, potsherds, and darkened postholes and foundation trenches. At Flag Fen, preservation is so perfect in the wetlands that you witness the remote past in all its real complexity. Looking down at the serried posts of successive walkways built over the centuries within a few feet of one another, you can imagine skin-clad families traversing the crude paths, dark posts on either side keeping the timbers and sand in place. The pathway is slippery, even on fine days, so that following it is sometimes a matter of finding your way from one beam in the mud to another. To left and right lie rows of posts projecting just above the murky water. A crossing farmer laden with firewood knows he will be up to his waist in mud if he tries to take a shortcut. Here, a crude dugout canoe lies alongside a narrow defile between the posts. In another place, a fishing basket hangs from a convenient sapling. Flag Fen reveals a complicated, pragmatic farming landscape of small fields, winding paths, and small thatched huts. It reveals it not as a series of sterile museum exhibits, or black-and white-lines on a plan in an archaeological mono-graph, but instead as an entire, abandoned yet luminous landscape. This is why wet sites, with their superior preservation conditions, are so important to us. More than any other kind of site, they show us just what the past was really like, almost down to the smells. Such sites are rare indeed, most of them like the 10,000-year-old camp at Star Carr in northeast England, which is just a few feet wide. By contrast, Flag Fen encompasses a sample of a vast Bronze Age landscape, reflecting the imprint of long-forgotten men and women over acres of an environment that no longer exists today. That is why waterlogged sites are so important, and why continued exca-vations at such sites will yield the richest dividends for the future. And that's why I will return to Flag Fen again and again—to remind myself just how profound has been the human imprint on an ancient landscape. ❈

PART II
COMMONERS, CAMELS, AND GREAT LORDS

The invention of writing in about 3000 B.C. gives modern archaeologists opportunities to work with another form of evidence for reconstructing the past—historical documents. At first, such written records were confined to king lists and formal inscriptions from Mesopotamia and Egypt. But within a thousand years the early civilizations developed literature and poetry, as well as complex archives of administrative and religious documents. Only a tiny minority of Sumerian and Egyptian citizens were literate in cuneifrom or hieroglyphs. The scribe was a member of a privileged class, exempt from the backbreaking labor of agriculture or public building works, which supported the state. Literacy was power. Most people still lived circumscribed lives, bound by the horizons of their fields, fellow kin, and community. It is here that archaeology comes into its own, for the material remains of the past form a dispassionate chronicle of the doings of anonymous, everyday folk far from the corridors of power. "The Humbler Egyptians" describes what we know about two Nile towns, the one a state-owned community used by mortuary workers, the other the royal capital of the heretic New Kingdom pharaoh Akhenaten. The archaeologists have used a combination of contemporary scripts and fieldwork to assemble portraits of common folk with close ties deep in the Egyptian countryside.

Transport on land and sea assumed ever greater importance in the ancient world. No animal was more important, yet has been more neglected by researchers, than the camel, domesticated between 2,000 and 3,000 years ago. As "Saddle Up the Camels!" points out, saddle design was as important as the beast itself. Being able to fight from high above the ground gave the desert nomad both immediate strategic advantage and political power. The load-carrying camel saddle opened up the Sahara to long-distance trade and linked Africa to Asia, West Africa to Europe, in an ever more complex web of interconnectedness that has culminated in the global economy of today.

The decipherment of Maya glyphs ranks among the most important scientific achievements of this century. "Readers in Maya" describes the decipherment process, the realization that the often grotesque glyphs represented phonetic syllables. Decipherment has enabled us to identify individual rulers, the buildings they built, and even the date of their reigns. Their inscriptions justify dynastic lines and serve as political propaganda. They reveal Maya lords not as peaceful priest-kings obsessed with astro- nomical observations and calendars, but instead as warlike, bloodthirsty rulers with a taste for conquest, intense competition, and human sacrifice.

Document-aided archaeology provides insights into the intangibles of early civilizations. In the case of the Maya, the glyphs reveal much of the complex symbolic world behind that civilization. Chinese records provide invaluable data on long-forgotten solar and lunar eclipses, which can be used to date major events in dynastic history. examined in "Dating by Solar Eclipse," eclipses are memorable events, not only for their astronomical significance, but as happenings in their own right, remembered for many generations. As the Chinese experience shows, they offer a valuable check of historical and archaeological datings.

Our society transmits knowledge from generation to generation in visual, written, and oral form. Non-literate societies like the Moche of coastal Peru relied on oral traditions as well as on an elaborate codification of their ideology broadcast on clay pots, textiles, and other artifacts. "The Magnificent Moche" tells the story of the Lords of Sipán, Peru, buried in great splendor under a high pyramid in coastal Peru in about A.D. 400. The richly decorated burial and formal regalia of these warrior-priests are mirrored in the painted friezes adorning hundreds of Moche pots. Archae- ologist Christopher Donnan used the ideology on these vessels to identify the burials as those of warrior-priests, who presided over ceremonies of war and human sacrifice.

Document-aided archaeology, sometimes called historical archaeology, provides a vital window into the centuries of recent history. "Brazil's Little Angola" describes a colony of escaped slaves who fled sugar plantations in northeastern Brazil and set up an independent community, Palmares, a safe distance away from their former masters. Palmares offers tantalizing possibilities for the archaeologist. Will it be possible to identify African artifacts at the site of the former settlement? To what extent did the inhabitants retain their African culture and means of governance? How did they settle across the landscape and grow their crops? Archaeology offers the potential for studying an independant African community in an alien land, and for examining the complex interactions both between the people of Palmares and local native American groups and between them and their European enemies.

Underwater archaeology has come into its own since the development of scuba diving equipment in World War II. "Balsa Rafts to Ironclads" surveys some of the major underwater archaeology discoveries in the Americas and assesses the potential of shipwrecks in illuminating major developments in recent history. ❁

CHAPTER NINE

THE HUMBLER EGYPTIANS

There are said to be 4,000 villages in modern Egypt, some with as many as 3,000 inhabitants. Land is in such short supply that houses huddle one against another in compact settlements lapped by waves of intensely cultivated fields. After centuries, even millennia, of continuous occupation, they stand above the level of the surrounding countryside. Before the Aswan Dam tamed the Nile, each village was a palm-fringed island surrounded by floodwaters at inundation time. Every time I sail up the Nile, a sense of timelessness settles over me, especially at sunset, when shapes are blurred and the people gather to gossip in the fading light. You gaze on scenes little changed from the days of the pharaohs. For more than 6,000 years, the Egyptians have tilled the fertile soils of their homeland, in an unchanging routine of planting and harvest. Great pharaohs rose and fell, conquered foreign lands, or faded before foreign masters. But village life along the Nile continued uninterrupted. It was no coincidence every Egyptian of city or town, whether high official, minor bureaucrat, or artisan, maintained close ties with the home village, with kin ties to the land and the countryside.

The pharaohs mesmerize us with their spectacular temples and endless invocations proclaiming their probity and piety. I find more than a few days spent viewing their monuments a trifle monotonous, for we see but the tip of the ancient Egyptian iceberg: the grandiose, rarefied life of great rulers and nobles. They headed a vast bureaucracy that reached down into the remotest villages. At times, too, officialdom created and administered small workers' communities for artisans building and decorating royal tombs or other public structures, which reveal much about the humbler members of Egyptian society. Far from spectacular, and usually off the tourist track, such settlements reveal the links between village and town, city-dweller and farmer.

The Middle Kingdom pharaohs ran a closely supervised bureaucracy that controlled every aspect of workers' lives. Enormous public structures and royal mortuaries required small armies of laborers, sometimes housed in special communities, some distance from their place of work. The Middle Kingdom town at Kahun (known to the Egyptians as Hetep-Senusret, "King Senusret is at peace") stood close to the entrance to the Fayum Depression in Lower Egypt, near the pyramid of Sesostris II. Here lived the priests and workers responsible for the king's mortuary cult, also people engaged in other construction works and agriculture. Kahun lay inside mudbrick walls, the interior laid out on a strict grid pattern of small houses and streets. Egyptologist Flinders Petrie uncovered a few intricately designed, fairly large houses with substantial granaries, in which household activities revolved around an inner court and walled garden. Much smaller houses outnumbered these residences by about 20:1, with an estimated 3,000 people living within the tightly packed community. The town plan reflects a society with well-defined social classes, reflected in house design as well as occupation.

Papyri found during Petrie's excavations reveal the existence of a mayor, legal offices, and a prison. They also contain census data, including those of the household of a mortuary priest with only one son and daughter, but many "serfs," some of them a product of his office, others domestic servants, "field laborers," cooks, tutors, and women who were "clothmakers" and gardeners. These groups of workers depended on the granaries of larger houses for their rations, thereby forming the economic teams that were so much a part of Egyptian society. Kahun's population also included scribes and soldiers, plus numerous small households of half a dozen people or more, many of them relatives and widows with dependent children.

Kahun represents the ultimate in Egyptian bureaucracy, a town laid out to fulfil a specific public need by high court officials with little conception of the realities of society. They organized Kahun at two levels: top officials, and others. In fact, the papyri reveal a more complex reality—of individuals and households wrestling with the demands of debt and children, of sudden inheritances and caring for the elderly. In truth, close kin ties between town and countryside were stronger than any draconian administration. It was no coincidence that New Kingdom administration was more decentralized, more relaxed. The stability of the state depended on it.

One New Kingdom city in particular has yielded a wealth of information: the heretic pharaoh Akhenaten's capital at El-Amarna, downstream of Thebes. Akhenaten ascended Egypt's throne in 1353 B.C., at a time when the Sun God Amun was all-powerful in the hands of the priesthood at Karnak in Thebes. Amun's power came through the age-old cult of Re Herakty, the primordial sun god of Heliopolis. His Great Disk, Aten, illuminated the worlds of the living and the dead. Akhenaten in effect demoted Amun and placed emphasis on Aten, excluding all the old gods of the pantheon from their association with Re Herakty. He made Aten a divine pharaoh, the equivalent in heaven of the living king on earth. We do not know why Akhenaten embarked from orthodoxy, but the art of his day suggests he regarded himself and his family as the sole intermediaries between the people and the sun-god. Akhenaten expected to be adored like a god and set out to distance himself from Thebes. In the fifth year of his reign, the heretic pharaoh founded a brand-new capital on land associated with no established deity. In so doing, he did a favor for archaeologists. El-Amarna was occupied for little more than a quarter century before being abandoned, leaving an Egyptian city of more than 20,000 inhabitants exposed under shallow deposits of sand instead of centuries of later occupation. Egyptologists from Flinders Petrie onward have used El-Amarna as a quite readable dictionary of ancient Egyptian city life.

The ceremonial precincts of El-Amarna revolved around a processional way that linked the North (Royal) City to the Central City. The fortified royal palace at the north end was isolated from the rest of El-Amarna. Here Akhenaten and his court resided in a self-sufficient, well-guarded community furnished with its own warehouses. The pharaoh rode grandly down the processional way on festival days, protected by his bodyguard as his subjects adulated him. The royal road ended at the Great Palace, a huge structure by the waterfront with a central courtyard where the king received emissaries and conducted many ceremonies, including the rewarding of high officials who were dependent on his largesse. The administrative functions of state were performed in offices attached to the Palace. It was here that the "Bureau for the Correspondence of the Pharaoh" lay, the archive that housed the now-famous Amarna diplomatic tablets that tell us so much about Egypt's diplomacy 3,500 years ago. The Great Temple of Aten stood close by.

But Amarna's greatest significance lies in its unique archaeological evidence for New Kingdom Egyptian society. Most Amarna residents lived in two large housing tracts north and south of the central city, huddled in small houses along streets parallel to the river, intersected by smaller alleys. Each flat-roofed dwelling stood in a small, walled compound amongst a maze of alleyways and garbage heaps. Each had a central living room with a low brick dais for receiving guests. Around the central space were reception rooms, bedrooms, and storage rooms. Wealthier people had larger houses, built to the same general design. We know the names of only a few individual owners, among them Ra-nefer, a chief charioteer, who lived in a modest house, while Thutmose was a sculptor who carried out his work in small courtyards by his house, in an area of the town devoted to sculptors. In the teeming city neighborhoods, papyri tell us how some prominent officials struggled to maintain a prosperous lifestyle, using income from their small country estates and donations from the king.

The houses of rich and poor are distinguished more by size than design. The greatest social chasm was between the pharaoh's court and the rest of society. El-Amarna's crowded houses were separated not by wide streets, but by narrow, winding alleyways through piles of domestic garbage, in urban communities where everyone lived cheek-by-jowl. The city was an aggregation of villages inhabited by people of similar occupations or with close kin ties, an element in a society that enjoyed great coherence. Except for the pharaoh and the highest court officials, the wealthy, for all their power and prestige, were part and parcel of ordinary life. The king and his entourage lived in a precinct of buildings remarkable for their grandeur and isolation. Their lives revolved around pageant, religious ritual, and servile adoration. Away from the palace, the pharaoh and his courtiers recede into the background, remembered only by the omnipresent statues and inscriptions that reminded everyone of divine and royal authority. The teeming city neighborhoods were home to officials struggling to balance their public duties with the need to keep in touch with their village roots. The smaller houses were home to lesser folk: servants, minor artisans, shopkeepers, boatmen, fisherfolk, and farmers. Busy people, idle folk, honest and dishonest citizens, free people and slaves—each pursued their individual goals, living close to the land, to the villages that provided the ultimate foundation of Egyptian life.

Ancient Egypt flourished in part because of massive government inter-vention in the agricultural economy and a relatively rational form of administration that maintained grain supplies and prices at stable levels over long periods of time. Its apparatus was crude, built around a powerful ideology for the glory of king and gods. In the end, the rulers faltered and vanished, as their state became more loosely structured and eventually fell apart. But the people survived, their roots firmly in village and countryside, their loyalties to kin and to the land rather than to transitory deities. ☀

CHAPTER TEN
SADDLE UP THE CAMELS!

Long before Islam reached North Africa in the seventh century A.D., heavily laden camels plodded south from Sijilmassa in Morocco to the African kingdom of Ghana on the southern edge of the desert. The caravans left each autumn, carrying cake salt from Saharan mines, as well as leather goods and woolen garments. Two months later, they arrived south of the desert in Ghana. Freshly watered and fattened, these same soft-footed beasts then plodded north, this time laden with gold, copper, ivory, kola nuts, and the other African raw materials that cake salt could buy.

For all their curmudgeonly temperament, camels are ideal for desert travel. They store fat in their humps. They have long necks that allow them to browse in trees and brush. Their padded feet allow them to walk on soft sand. Contrary to popular belief, the camel does not store water, it conserves it through an efficient kidney system and can distribute immense amounts of water through its body tissue within 48 hours. At the same time, these remarkable animals can absorb heat by allowing their body temperature to rise six degrees above normal in the course of a single day without perspiring. They are ideal beasts of burden.

Camels were probably first domesticated in southern Arabia sometime before 2500 B.C., but more than ten centuries were to pass before they came into common use. Why, one might ask, did the camel not immediately revolutionize desert travel in the Near East? The problem was the saddle.

The first Arabian camel saddles were mounted over the animals' hindquarters. Seated near the rear of the beast, the rider had to use a stick to control his mount, and he also lost the major strategic advantage of the camel—the height of his master above the ground.

The first breakthrough came with the development of the North Arabian saddle during the five centuries before Christ. This is a rigid, arched seat mounted over the camel's hump that distributes the rider's weight evenly; not on the hump, but on the beast's back. A pack load could be slung on either side of the saddle. More important, a warrior could fight from camelback with sword or spear. The North Arabian saddle suddenly gave camel-breeding nomads new economic and political power.

The result of this invention was a dramatic, but initially inconspicuous, shift in the balance of commercial and political power over much of the Near East. Originally, control of the precious Arabian trade resided with the buyers and producers of frankincense and other commodities. King Solomon was a buyer, the Queen of Sheba—with her "very great train, with camels that bore spices, and very much gold, and precious stones"—a seller. Both waxed rich on the camel-borne trade; the owners of the beasts themselves were unimportant. Now the camel breeders found themselves in the proverbial saddle, as the profits flowed into their hands. Petra in the Jordanian desert was the first of the great caravan cities. Wheeled carts effectively vanished from the Near Eastern world for many centuries. The camel with a North Arabian saddle was more efficient.

Large numbers of camels first arrived in Egypt when Assyrians and then Persians invaded the land of the pharaohs in the seventh and sixth centuries B.C. Generations later, during the second and first centuries B.C., Egyptian records speak of camel caravans that traveled the 500 miles between the Red Sea and Upper Egypt. Nevertheless, wheeled transport was still important along the river. As late as the first century B.C., the Greek geographer Strabo traveled through the Nile Valley in a carriage. By this time, the power and presence of the eastern desert nomads was on the increase. Camel-breeding nomads such as the Beja of the northeastern Sudan dominated the lucrative trade routes that linked the Red Sea with the Nile. They had acquired camels and North Arabian saddles from across the Red Sea, probably from Arabian caravan operators working trade routes between Petra and Leuce Come, a Red Sea port opposite the Egyptian harbor at Myus Hormos.

The first-century B.C. kingdom of Meroe in the present-day Sudan also profited greatly from the camel. Meroe was an iron-working state that lay on the Nile at a great crossroads, where trade routes from Egypt, the Ethiopian highlands, and the Red Sea met. The rulers of Meroe supplied war elephants for Rome's armies, and exported gold, ivory and other raw materials to Red Sea ports along desert routes that were now camel highways. From Meroe, new camel tracks stretched westward into the seemingly endless Sahara.

The first mention of the camel in North Africa comes from Caesar's account of his campaign against Juba in southern Tunisia in 46 B.C. Caesar captured 22 camels from the Numidian king, a small number for the animal was still rare in these parts. During the next three centuries the camel population multiplied, so much so that the Romans placed a requisition of no less than 4,000 animals on the city of Leptus Magna in Tripolitania in A.D. 363. But the Romans did not use the camel for desert travel. Instead, they set them to work pulling carts and employed them to form defensive corrals for foot soldiers—the Sahara was the southern frontier of the Roman Empire, a vast sea of sand inhabited by nomadic Berbers who preyed constantly on settled Roman lands.

French scholar Theodore Monod, who has spent many years on the esoteric topic of Saharan camel saddles, has identified three distinct design types, each of which is mounted on the camel's shoulders, forward of the hump. These were not military saddles, for which height of the rider was essential, both for visibility and use of weaponry. Rather they were so positioned as to maximize load-carrying capacity, endurance, and easy control on long marches. This saddle was ideal for the Sahara for the driver could steer the beast effortlessly with a stick or his toes. All three types developed in areas where there were no Roman cavalry or other enemies to worry about. When these new saddle designs made really long-distance travel practicable, the intricate tentacles of long-distance trade routes from the east reached deep into the Sahara and eventually into North Africa. And from Meroe and Dongola, too, caravan routes now extended far west along the southern margins of the Sahara to West Africa. For centuries, the Saharan saddle carried peaceful loads across the desert. It was not until the seventh century A.D. that Arab armies introduced the North Arabian military saddle to the desert. By that time the camel had become the "ship of the desert," the vehicle of a lucrative trade in Saharan cake salt, so highly prized in West Africa that chiefs would pay for it with the equivalent weight in gold. Thus it was that the ingeniously designed camel saddle became one of the great catalysts of African history. ✹

CHAPTER ELEVEN

READERS IN MAYA

Imagine studying American history with no other documentary sources than each president's State of the Union messages. The epigrapher Linda Schele uses this apt analogy to describe the challenge Mayanists face as they unlock the secrets of ancient Maya glyphs. At first glance, a State of the Union message appears incomplete and, because of its very purpose, somewhat slanted in both viewpoint and content. Thus, it can seem an unsatisfactory historical source. In fact, the presidential speeches are full of intricate symbolism, important references, and basic policy statements. They reflect the contemporary concerns of society at large. Carefully dissected and analyzed, they can yield a remarkable amount of information about the society to which they were addressed. The messages from Maya glyphs are as complicated and fascinating.

The story of how we reached our current understanding of the glyphs is complicated and fascinating as well. Until recently, Maya was one of the few ancient scripts—such as Etruscan and the crabbed writing of the Harappan civilization of the Indus—that continued to defy Western scholarship. Now that the ancient Maya glyphs have begun to yield their secrets, our understanding of Mesoamerican civilization stands to be revolutionized. Today the field of Maya studies is at a critical threshold . . . but that is getting ahead of the story.

Like so many great scholarly feats, Maya decipherment was long in coming and largely ignored when it came. In the 1950s, the Soviet researcher Yuri Knorozov, himself following the lead of earlier German and American colleagues, published pioneering work on the phonetics of ancient Maya, work that was to prove pivotal in later decipherment. However, many Mayanists such as Tatiana Proskouriakoff and J. Eric Thompson did not accept his ideas. Knorozov's work was disregarded for more than 35 years except by a few scholars such as David Kelley and the linguist Floyd Lounsbury, today the doyen of Maya glyph studies. For years, they were voices crying in the academic wilderness.

From the turn of the century, some scholars such as Herbert Spinden argued that Maya glyphs were not only calendrical but important historical and genealogical records as well. It is astounding in retrospect that almost the entire Mayanist community refused to accept such theories. It was as if their research were divorced from historical reality. They could not accept that Maya civilization and history were like those of the rest of humanity—that the Maya, like any other early civilization, were people who had fought wars, settled disputes with diplomacy, and cherished their history. Then, in a classic paper for American Antiquity in 1960, Tatiana Proskouriakoff demonstrated beyond all reasonable doubt that Spinden and other pioneers had been right. The glyphs were indeed a chronicle of great families and events of Maya history, not merely calendrical and astronomical records. Maya studies were transformed almost overnight.

Decipherment did not come easily, however, partly because scholars were approaching it by different avenues of inquiry. When archaeologists, epigraphers, and linguists working on Maya glyphs gathered in Mexico City for a conference in 1966, the various factions, lacking a common vocabulary, barely communicated with one another. The problem of non-communication was compounded by the fact that relatively few people—led by Heinrich Berlin, Knorozov, and Proskouriakoff—were actively working in Maya script at the time. Others became involved by accident. Floyd Lounsbury, for example, began his fascination with glyphs when he was asked, by chance, to review some early articles on the subject. He studied individual glyphs in an attempt to understand the syntax of Maya script—words, subjects, objects, and their order.

Into the early 1970s, the situation remained unsatisfactory, as the different camps applied their own—frequently narrow—methods and goals to Maya decipherment. However, there comes a moment in many scholarly endeavors when things achieve what one might call a critical mass, when great advances are made by a single inspired gesture or as a result of intense discussion. The turning point for the Mayanists came at two meetings in 1973 and 1974. The first was at Palenque in Mexico, where the discussions about glyphs opened up the field to a whole new generation of young scholars, with multidisciplinary perspectives, who would themselves one day train newcomers. Elizabeth P. Benson, then director of the Dumbarton Oaks Center for Pre-Columbian Studies, in Washington, D.C., was at the Palenque meeting and saw that a moment of truth was nigh, that a suitable environment was needed for intensive discussion between scholars with different specialties. She organized the first in what would become a series of seminars on Maya glyphs at Dumbarton Oaks the following year. Again because the scholars lacked a common ground for discussion, that first meeting ended in exasperated deadlock. In frustration, the epigrapher Linda Schele, now of the University of Texas, corralled Floyd Lounsbury and rolled out a long sequence of Palenque glyphs on the seminar room carpet. David Kelley, Peter Mathews, and Merle Robertson joined them on the floor. Two and a half hours later, the group had refined the first few hundred years of the Palenque dynasty's history.

Until the ferment that began at Dumbarton Oaks in 1974, most analyses had concentrated on individual glyphs, on the decipherment of single signs. People felt it was necessary to explain every context of each glyph in order to understand them. After the Dumbarton Oaks meetings, Lounsbury argued that the glyphs were not just signs, they were a *spoken* language, so word order was critical, as was the broad structural analysis of the script. This approach enabled Lounsbury and his followers to place individual glyphs in the context of syntax. Following Knorozov, they presumed the glyphs were not mnemonic devices, aids to recitation, but phonetic elements of a spoken language with grammar, syntax, and specific rules of order. Once they had stepped over this critical hurdle, the path to decipherment opened up.

Maya glyph studies are now rapidly coming of age, evolving into a respected field of epigraphy whose practitioners work with real, complex scripts. Since the pioneer days of the 1970s, the slowly growing coterie of "glyphers" has gone off in several different directions, but they have many common ties. Many experts specialize in Maya linguistics, working on discovering structural patterns that will aid in further decipherments. Others have a strong historical orientation and are working to recover both Maya histories and religious beliefs. Decipherment per se is a secondary goal, although the various specialists work closely together, going over texts again and again seeking new insights. What is most important is the context of the glyphs and their cultural implications.

Linda Schele believes Maya epigraphy is at the same threshold reached by scholars of Near Eastern languages a century ago. The choice is fundamentally simple: either pursue epigraphy for its own sake, focusing on a detached, highly specialized field that is a world unto its own, or retain an important presence in the mainstream of Maya studies. Retaining such a presence means continuing a strong tradition in epigraphy—the tradition of the epigrapher working in the field alongside the anthropologist-archaeologist. This "marriage" between excavator and glyph expert, as the brilliant young epigrapher David Stuart calls it, starts in the field, continues in the laboratory, and should persist over long periods of time. Not that the marriage is confined to archaeologists. "Us glyphers will marry anybody," says Schele with enthusiasm.

By no means have all Maya archaeologists adjusted to a new research environment in which historical texts and genealogies will increasingly serve as valuable sources for insights into Maya life. Some of them have felt for many years that both Maya art, with its intricate visual symbolism, and the accompanying script are best treated as entirely separate subdisciplines, just as they have been in classical archaeology for generations. This is a strangely myopic view of the archaeological record, for it ignores the glyphs and texts as primary sources of information about the past.

Mayanists such as Linda Schele and the archaeologist David Friedel are trying to combine both state-of-the-art anthropological archaeology and all the sophistication of Maya philology into a seamless, interdisciplinary record of Maya civilization. They argue that students of the Maya civilization should use primary data from any legitimate source. They are working to produce an "anthropological history" of the Maya, a history that combines information from glyphs with interpretations of culture change derived from archaeological fieldwork. For example, they have thrown new light on the conquest of Uaxactun by Tikal in 437, and on Tikal's remarkable recovery from its defeat at the hands of Caracol in Belize on May 1, 562.

In an effort to nip intellectual myopia and a retreat to "old-fashioned" Maya studies in the bud, Anabel Ford of the University of California at Santa Barbara organized an interdisciplinary conference in March 1988. The conference, entitled "The Language of Maya Hieroglyphs," brought together not only linguists and epigraphers from all over North America and farther afield, but archaeologists and ethnohistorians as well. All of them realized that our knowledge of Maya civilization can no longer come from any one source.

The Santa Barbara conference demonstrated once again what a pity it would be if Maya epigraphers went one way and the archaeologists another. The past 15 years have seen a series of quiet revolutions in Maya epigraphy. It is only now that we archaeologists can fully understand the extent of the epigraphers' brilliant achievement. Clearly, this is a "marriage" that ought not end in divorce. ☀

CHAPTER TWELVE

DATING BY SOLAR ECLIPSE

"**D**uring the first year of the reign of King Yi, in the first month of spring, the sun rose twice at Zheng," the Chinese chronicle reads. What can a scientist make of a statement like that? It took UCLA historian Hung-hsiang Chou and Cal Tech astronomer Kevin Pang two years to figure it out. They did so by matching ancient astronomical records with space age computer simulations for the movements of the earth and moon. Their results yielded both a date for the double sunrise, i.e., eclipse—April 21, 899 B.C.—and an intriguing new way of dating ancient Chinese civilization.

The foundation for Chou and Pang's success however, was laid thousands of years ago. Three legendary dynasties of early Chinese civilization—the Xia, Shang, and Zhou—presided over powerful and competitive states centered on the Yellow River valley of northern China more than 3,000 years ago. We know little of their shadowy rulers. They did record their deeds on bamboo strips, but a successor, Emperor Shi Huang Di (221–209 B.C.), the first ruler of all China and among the most dictatorial, ordered all such archives destroyed.

Only a handful of these ancient chronicles survived, among them the so-called *Bamboo Annals*. Hidden away in the tomb of King Hsiang in the third century B.C., they survived both the emperor Shi Huang Di and the attention of tomb robbers. In the third century A.D., they were salvaged by Emperor Wu, a man far more respectful of the past than his predecessor, Shi Huang Di. He set scholars to work sorting and collating the wagonloads of archival bamboo strips retrieved from the tomb, a task that took years. Thirteen chapters of these records make up the *Bamboo Annals*. A chronology of important events in ancient times, they provided vital records for early Chinese civilization.

For more than 4,000 years, the Chinese have kept astonishingly accurate astronomical records, an academic and intellectual tradition that survives to this day. Beijing Observatory has already published an astounding compilation of 1.5 million words on astronomy, drawn from more than 150,000 historical texts. In historical times, Chinese astronomers duly recorded all but two of the 30 appearances of Halley's Comet. Their records of 1,600 solar and 1,100 lunar eclipses have proved as complete. There is every reason to believe that their more ancient predecessors were just as precise. One of the earliest recorded observations by Chinese astronomers was of a total eclipse of the sun that occurred on October 16, 1876 B.C.

Archaeologists as well as historians are aware of the dating potential of ancient eclipse records. However, the study of ancient eclipses bristles with historiographical difficulties. Early observers couched their descriptions of such phenomena in mysterious, even mystical terms. For example, the expression "the sky rained blood" is found in both Chinese and European texts and is probably inspired by the deep color of Red Type A auroras. "The day dawned twice" may be a similar kind of exaggeration, a description of a total solar eclipse that occurs just before dawn.

One can date an eclipse by establishing the positions of the earth and moon relative to the sun, but the locations on earth where it might have been seen depend on the rotational history of the earth. Over time, the earth's spin rate has slowed. Moreover, the continual recession of the moon from the earth has also affected the places and times where eclipses could be seen. While the moon's recession rate has been measured by laser and is generally assumed to be constant, the slowdown in the earth's rotation rate is variable due to many complex factors, including sea level changes and the melting of ice sheets.

Meanwhile, Chinese astronomical records are deficient in several other important respects. Most commonly, like many other such records, they tend to be vague about the location, magnitude, and time of the eclipse. King Yi's document is especially valuable, for it places the time of the eclipse at sunrise, obviating the need for a precise time calculation, and it locates it at a precise point, the town of Zheng . . . . Which brings us back to California, and to the work of Chou and Pang.

Eclipses observed at sunset or sunrise provide reliable data about the time of day, which makes them especially useful in calculating the Earth's spin rate. In matching King Yi's sunrise eclipse and other Chinese astronomical records with computer simulations of the movements of earth and moon, Chou and Pang were able to determine the earth's gradually slowing rotation rate to within thousandths of a second. For example, they calculated that, compared with today, the length of a day was 22 thousandths of a second shorter in A.D. 532; 42 thousandths of a second shorter in 899 B.C.; and 60 thousandths of a second briefer in 1876 B.C. Using the same simulations, they then sought to establish the dates of several important events in early Chinese history.

Their first task was to sort through thousands of Chinese eclipse records and to choose one that matched approximately known historical events. They picked King Yi's "double dawn." By using archaeological finds such as oracle bones and bronze inscriptions to verify the royal genealogies of the Shang and Zhou dynasties, Chou and Pang were able to estimate the length of a generation to be 30 years. Since the records tell that King Yi ruled two generations before 841 B.C., the first accurately known date in Chinese history, this calculation placed the beginning of his reign at about 901 B.C. They then used the computers of the Jet Propulsion Laboratory in Pasadena, California, to simulate the movement of the earth and moon backward toward the "double dawn." Eventually, they found only one eclipse whose path lined up with the city of Zheng. If the day then had been as long as it is now, the eclipse would not have occurred over Zheng but would have been seen in the Near East 5 hours and 48 minutes later. But the computers enabled the two scholars to factor in the slower rotation, making the day 42 thousandths of a second shorter in King Yi's time—and placed the eclipse over Zheng at sunrise on April 21, 899 B.C.

The researchers then went further back into Chinese history to analyze the oldest recorded Chinese eclipse of all. According to the *Bamboo Annals*, the eclipse was observed during the fifth year of the reign of King Zhong Kang, the fourth king of the Xia dynasty, the earliest of the famous three Dynasties of early Chinese civilization. The eclipse took place on "the first day of the last month of autumn." We are told that "the blind musicians beat their drums, and the lower-ranked officers and common people bustled and ran about." This earliest of eclipse records contained some vital clues. It cites the last month of autumn, which in the Xia calendar was about the same month as our own October. Not only that, but it says the eclipse was seen in that portion of the sky known as lunar mansion Fang, corresponding with the approximate location of the constellation Scorpio. There were hundreds of eclipses recorded within a few centuries of Zhong Kang's reign, but only one was visible from Xia domains in October, and that was located exactly in the middle of Fang. The computers produced a date of October 16, 1876 B.C., putting the beginning of Zhong Kang's reign in the year 1880 B.C.

There were no earlier eclipse records, but in their study of documentary sources, Chou and Pang chanced upon the mention of an unusual clustering of five bright planets in the *Xiao Jing Gou Ming Jue*, a compilation of astronomical writings from the second century B.C. The text said that "at the beginning of the Xia dynasty, the five planets lined up clearly like a string of pearls, brightly burning like joined jade disks." This time, the computer revealed that Jupiter, Venus, Mercury, Mars, and Saturn did indeed cluster in the sky above the Xia capital of Yangcheng on February 23, 1953 B.C. in a nearly straight line.

Chou and Pang's conclusions have been confirmed by David Pankenier, a specialist in Chinese history at Lehigh University. He not only confirms the date of 1953 B.C. for the beginning of the Xia dynasty but has used a similar technique to propose a date of 1059 B.C. for the fall of the Shang Dynasty, and a date of about 1579 B.C. for the end of the Xia.

There are, of course, enormous difficulties in using ancient scripts to date ancient eclipses, for the crabbed texts are full of miscopyings, spelling errors, and symbolic allusions. These distortions notwithstanding, ancient astronomical phenomena offer one of the few ways in which we may hope to date the beginnings of Chinese civilization with any confidence. All of which goes to support the old truism that archaeology is one of those disciplines that flourishes on the arcane joining of obscure specialties. In this particular case, the academic marriage is likely to be long and happy. ✸

CHAPTER THIRTEEN
THE MAGNIFICENT MOCHE

The royal tombs of Sipán, excavated by Walter Alva in the heart of the ancient Moche kingdom on Peru's north coast, rank among this century's most spectacular archaeological discoveries (see *Archaeology*, November/December 1992 and September/October 1993). Until recently, few people outside Peru had the opportunity to see these magnificent artifacts. Now a collaborative effort by UCLA's Fowler Museum of Cultural History, the Brüning Museum in Lambayeque, and the Peruvian government has brought these remarkable antiquities to North Americans. For the next two years, the exhibition *Royal Tombs of Sipán* will tour the United States. The proceeds of the show will enable the Brüning Museum to build a permanent home for the treasures.

The Moche kingdom was a small polity by the standards of, say, ancient Egypt or the Aztec empire of Mexico. Between the first and eighth centuries A.D. Moche lords presided over a series of coastal river valleys spanning a north-south distance of about 350 miles. The Moche were masters of irrigation farming and fishing. They traded with people living far beyond the narrow confines of their own state, importing lapis lazuli from Chile and valuable *Spondylus* shells from Ecuador. Moche lords treasured tropical bird feathers and forest animals such as monkeys and boa constrictors. Like other ancient Andean rulers, they received food from their subjects and redistributed this wealth to nobles of lesser rank. Enormous food surpluses supported full-time artisans, who created rare and prestigious objects for a privileged nobility. Though Moche craftspeople were expert weavers and metalworkers, they were, above all, potters, arguably the best in Pre-Columbian America. They developed techniques not only for molding and stamping clay vessels, but also for painting complex scenes on bowls, pots, and vessels. Their artists painted intricate scenes of elaborately costumed figures engaged in hunting, fighting, and important religious ceremonies. Many of the finest pots have ended up in private U.S. collections. Until the excavations at Sipán, Moche archaeology was a frustrating salvage operation. Much of our knowledge of the Moche was based on looted artifacts rather than study of undisturbed graves or stratified village sites.

Christopher Donnan, director of the Fowler Museum and a leading authority on Moche art, iconography, and ceramics, has spent his entire career studying these ceramics, building a photographic archive of all known Moche vessels, whether in private or public collections. His research is a combination of detective and salvage work—tracking down vanished masterpieces and poring over three-dimensional portrait jars kept in private collections and storerooms. Donnan has been criticized for befriending collectors and studying their collections, on the grounds that such activity by archaeologists encourages even more frenzied looting. In fact Donnan is quietly making sure the work of Moche potters survives the vagaries of private collections and individual ownership where one generation may not value what previous ones cherished. Donnan's position is difficult. To completely ignore artifacts in private hands is to risk their permanent loss. To publish or authenticate them could, however, increase the value of individual pieces and increase demand.

Donnan's years of research, coupled with the Sipán discoveries, have paid off. He has cracked the preliterate iconographic "code" of Moche life. There are no glyphs on Moche vessels to tell their story and as far as we know they never practiced writing. Instead, researchers like Donnan look closely at minute stylistic details, costumes, and individual scenes. Warriors and their activities figure large on the pots. Donnan has recorded processions of warriors carrying clubs and other weapons; men engaged in one-on-one combat in barren desert landscapes; and prisoners arraigned before an important individual, prior to being sacrificed, their blood consumed, and their bodies dismembered. Donnan believes the Moche went to war to capture victims for an important sacrifice ceremony that they depicted again and again in their art. He has studied the figures shown attending the ceremony and identified some of them, most important a Warrior-Priest wearing a crescent-shaped headdress atop a conical helmet. Donnan's theory that the sacrifice ceremony was an integral part of Moche life and not a mythological scene was confirmed by Alva's excavation of a

Warrior-Priest, now known as the Lord of Sipán, wearing, as Donnan predicted, a conical helmet and crescent-shaped headdress. Still further excavations at Sipán, and subsequently in the Jequetepeque Valley to the north, revealed the burials of yet more participants in the sacrifice ceremony. All of these individuals correspond to figures depicted on Moche vases. These nobles, living in different parts of the kingdom, enacted the sacrifice ceremony at prescribed times. When they died, they were buried at the place where they had performed the rite, wearing the formal regalia and objects they used in the ritual. Their successors assumed their roles, wearing new sets of the same costumes and regalia, perpetuating the state religion and assuring work for the dozens of skilled artisans who manufactured objects for the nobility.

When Donnan invited me to visit the exhibition in its temporary home at the Fowler Museum, I leapt at the opportunity. I had heard about the exquisite workmanship of the artifacts, but nothing prepared me for the darkened galleries resplendent with necklaces of gold and silver peanut beads, golden disks, anthropomorphized crabs, and golden eye and nose ornaments—to name just a few.

Fittingly, the Sipán exhibit starts with line drawings of scenes depicted on some of Donnan's pots alongside delicately painted ceramic vessels illustrated with warriors and the sacrifice ceremony. The Lords of Sipán ruled over a society with ideologies and religious beliefs as powerful, and constraining, as those of ancient Egyptian pharaohs or the rulers of Aztec Tenochtitlán. One then enters galleries overflowing with gold and silver artifacts. Wall displays show the grave goods, flattened and corroded, as Alva uncovered them. One marvels at the patience of the Peruvian and German conservators who labored for months on the tiny ornaments and necklaces. One lord wore exquisitely crafted bracelets made of hundreds of minute beads of turquoise, shell, and gold, strung with copper spacer bars. Alva lifted these intact, using unspun cotton batting and soluble glue, then restored them to their original state. The Peruvians have achieved miracles of conservation with the slenderest of resources, an accomplishment for which they deserve our undying gratitude.

What manner of men were these lords? How did lesser Moche view them? At the end of the exhibit one confronts designer David Mayo's masterpiece—a model of the Lord of Sipán staring serenely into the distance, caparisoned in a long tunic covered with square platelets of gilded copper, with copper cones at the fringe. He wears a belt with crescent-shaped bells and a warrior's golden backflap. A large crescent-shaped headdress looms high from the woven conical hat on his head. The lord carries a gold and silver scepter in his right hand. The model moves from right to left, the gold and copper shimmering brilliantly in the overhead lights.

Sadly, to judge by the artifacts that have appeared on the art market in recent years, many Moche tombs have been lost. But on this occasion the Warrior-Priests have triumphed. Buried for more than 1,500 years in the dessicated mounds of Sipán, the Lords and their treasures came to light through a rigorous process of scientific excavation. One can only hope the message they bring will not be lost on those who consider the past a gold mine, rather than our collective cultural heritage. ☼

CHAPTER FOURTEEN
BRAZIL'S LITTLE ANGOLA

At last we are moving beyond the concept of historical archaeology as simply a means of chronicling daily life in urban settings, rural towns, missions, and mining settlements. A few innovative projects are now reaching far beyond the boundaries of individual communities to study the relationships of settlements not only to close neighbors, but to a much wider universe of nations and continents linked by economic networks that brought people from many cultures, most of them anonymous laborers, to new lands. This is the archaeology not only of the Atlantic slave trade, but of ethnic diversity in towns and villages throughout the Americas, of people from widely different cultural backgrounds who dealt with each other on a daily basis. The intricacies of these relationships are the meat and drink of some emerging, cutting-edge research. We have long needed a laboratory to test the potential of such inquiry. The seventeenth-century kingdom of Palmares established by runaway slaves in northeastern Brazil may be just such a laboratory.

Portuguese caravels made landfall on the low-lying northeastern Brazilian coast in 1500. The rich soils of the coastal plain were ideal for the large-scale cultivation of sugar cane. The Portuguese, who were already growing sugar on slave plantations on the Canary Islands and Madeira, developed similar farms in Brazil and imported enslaved Africans to work them. Over the next four centuries, more slaves were exported from West and central Africa to Brazil than to anywhere else in the Americas, perhaps as many as 4,000 a year. By 1627, there were no fewer than 230 sugar mills in Brazil, 170 along the northeastern coast. Since birth rates among enslaved Africans were low, and the average productive life of a sugar worker was about seven years, the plantation owners were forever buying new captives. Inevitably, some of them escaped into the interior.

Palmares was founded in about 1605 by 40 central Africans. Escaping slavery, they fled into heavily forested hills that parallel the northeastern coast, where they created a free settlement they called Angola janga (Little Angola), perhaps after their distant homeland. In time, it would become the largest community of runaway slaves, or maroons, in the Americas. The Portuguese were well aware of the settlement and named it Palmares, because of its many palm trees. Portuguese planters, however, regarded it as a rival and mounted an abortive attack on its inhabitants in 1612. Palmares continued to be a thorn in the Portuguese side, for its intent was "to rob the Portuguese of their slaves, who remain in slavery among them until they have redeemed themselves by stealing another," Dutchman John Nieuhoff tells us in his *Voyages and Travels into Brazil*. By all accounts, they did a good job of it, welcoming hundreds of escapees into their ranks.

By 1640, the Dutch had taken over the sugar plantations as part of an aggressive assault on Portuguese overseas interests. An expedition under Dutch colonist Bartolomeus Lintz was sent to scout out their increasingly aggressive maroon neighbor. He described two settlements, one a town of three streets and about 1,000 inhabitants living in small grass cabins. At least 5,000 more maroons lived on small holdings in two fertile valleys. According to Lintz, the people subsisted off "dates, beans, meal, barley, sugarcanes, tame-fowl (of which they have great plenty), and fish." Palmares was now such a threat that the Dutch returned with a force of native Brazilians and destroyed one major settlement with "iron and fire." The next year, they besieged a town fortified with a double palisade and a trench lined with sharpened stakes. Inside lay 200 houses, a church, four iron forges, and a large council house. The assault was to no avail, because Phoenix-like Palmares rose again. Between 1670 and 1694, it became a small kingdom with as many as 20,000 inhabitants living in ten villages scattered over about 106 miles of hinterland country. They were ruled by a leader named Ganga Zumba (Great Lord), who lived at the capital village, Macaco, probably the settlement attacked by the Dutch in 1645. Ultimately the Palmarinos were more successful than the Dutch, who abandoned Brazil, leaving it in the hands of the Portuguese.

By 1672, the authorities had lost patience with Palmares and attacked it repeatedly. Ganga Zumba, who had sought to live peacefully alongside the Portuguese, was murdered in 1687 by his nephew Zumbi, who was far more aggressive in his resistance to the Portuguese. Tension rose rapidly. The colonists mounted an expedition of ferocious Brazilian fighters against Macaco in 1694. It took 42 days to destroy the kingdom. In February 1694, the final assault on Macaco ended in vicious hand-to-hand combat. Some 200 Palmarinos died in battle and 200 more were killed when they jumped over a cliff in the confusion of flight. About 500 more "of both sexes and all ages" were captured and sold into slavery. Zumbi was decapitated, his head displayed in public to "kill the legend of immortality." The greatness of Palmares was never duplicated, for the Portuguese had learned their lesson. They organized special military units to hunt for fledgling maroon communities and nip them in the bud. They also dispersed incoming slaves into widely separated communities, to guard against solidarity.

Today, African-Brazilians hail Zumbi as a hero of Brazilian history. Bars, restaurants, even auto parts stores are named after him. Palmares itself has become a major symbol of African-Brazilian cultural identity. And Macaco and other Palmarino settlements are among the most important sites in Brazil, with unlimited potential for unraveling the complex relationships between Portuguese and Palmarino, between maroons and native Americans.

Excavations began last year under the supervision of an international team of archaeologists, headed by Brazilian Pedro Funari, Englishman Michael Rowlands, and American Charles E. Orser, Jr. They located no fewer than ten sites at Macaco alone during their first field survey. Surface finds were mainly fine-bodied, untempered ceramics and shreds of Portuguese, tin-glazed majolica. When sorted, they comprised at least four kinds of ceramics, which represent, perhaps, what Brazilian historian Decio Freitas calls a "cultural mosaic" that united elements of African, native Brazilian, and perhaps even Portuguese and Dutch colonial culture. Herein lies the great archaeological potential of Palmares, for, theoretically, it should be possible to clarify some of the intricate relationships between Palmarino and native American, Palmarino and settler, and even between men and women at Palmares itself, simply by studying artifacts.

Unfortunately, relations among the various groups were not as straightforward as one might expect. For example, Portuguese colonial society was not united in its opposition to Palmares. The rich plantation owners and merchants hated the upstart kingdom. But it had the support of humbler settlers inland, who traded firearms to Palmarinos in blatant defiance of the colonial government and the church. In exchange they received ample supplies of cane, bananas, and beans. The same colonists tipped off their neighbors about impending attacks. Then there were the Tupinamba, native Brazilian farmers, who were quickly enslaved by the Portuguese, but who died by the thousands to be replaced by Africans. We know that the Portuguese employed some Indians as mercenaries in attacks on Palmares, but others living nearby may have enjoyed close relationships with the maroon communities. There are tantalizing hints of such relationships in the form of thick-bodied, heavily tempered Native American vessels found at Macaco alongside majolica wares. Since Tupinamba pottery is made by women, such finds offer exciting opportunities for studying gender relations at Palmares, situations somewhat akin to those at Spanish St. Augustine in Florida, where some Spanish settlers lived in households whose material culture was significantly Indian, perhaps because they had married Indian women.

"He has a palatial residence, *casas* for members of his family, and is assisted by guards and officials, who have, by custom, houses which approach those of royalty. He is treated with all respect due a Monarch and all the honors due a Lord. Those who are in his presence kneel on the ground and strike palm leaves with their hands . . . ." The "Great Lord" of Palmares ruled in considerable grandeur and, we are told, with an iron hand. His was a centralized kingdom, the principal offices going to his relatives. A question arises: was this remarkable kingdom based on African proto-types in distant Angola in central Africa, the homeland of most of the original Palmarinos? The answer seems to be that Palmares was a mosaic of influences from several African kingdoms. Here, again, the potential for archaeology is enormous, for such artifacts as iron balls, anvils, or brass ornaments are important symbols of kingship in Africa. Were such artifacts manufactured in Brazil? Did the escaped Africans re-create their society from memory, duplicating institutions that had governed people effectively in their homeland? Do their artifacts reflect not only their African heritage but complex cultural borrowings and relationships with both Native Americans and European colonists? Only the large-scale excavations that are planned at Palmares can answer these questions. It is good news that they are in expert, international hands, for Palmares promises not only to revolutionize African-Brazilian history but also to demonstrate the enormous potential of archaeology as a tool for studying the African diaspora, for answering questions that interest not only archaeologists and historians, but African-Americans as well. ❧

CHAPTER FIFTEEN

BALSA RAFTS
TO IRONCLADS

C aptain Nathaniel Basse arrived by ship at Jamestown on April 27, 1619. This, in itself, was hardly a momentous event in archaeological history, until you realize that nautical archaeologist George Bass may be one of his progeny. Bass is also descended from Algonkian-speaking Indians, and his great-great-grandfather drowned in a steamboat wreck, so his interest in the watercraft of North America runs deep. In a real sense, George is "Mr. Nautical Archaeology," though he would be the first to give credit to his many colleagues exploring ancient shipwrecks around the globe. It is not surprising that many of them were trained at the Institute of Nautical Archaeology, founded by Bass at Texas A & M University in 1973.

Over 25 years ago George edited *A History of Seafaring Based on Underwater Archaeology* (Thames & Hudson, London, 1970), a seminal volume combining historical information with rapidly emerging archaeological data. *A History* was an immediate bestseller, by archaeological standards, and was translated into six languages. Major emphasis in the book was placed on the early ships and boats of the Mediterranean and Northern Europe, with only two chapters dealing with the watercraft of the Americas.

In 1988, George compiled another important and comprehensive volume, *Ships and Shipwrecks of the Americas* (Thames & Hudson, New York, 1988). Lavishly illustrated, the book addresses all aspects of maritime activity in the Americas, from the balsa raft and birch canoe to the great sailing ships and ironclads of the nineteenth century. Watercraft of all kinds have played a major role in shaping human life, Bass tells us, adding that, unfortunately, our knowledge of these vessels, their construction, and the people who built and used them remains tantalizingly incomplete.

For many years a few dedicated scholars like the late Howard Chapelle, of the Smithsonian Institution, have pursued decaying work boats all over North America, documenting their lines and often supervising the construction of replicas. In fact, somewhat of an addiction to marine restoration and maritime museums has exploded on these shores in recent years, a development that is not always accompanied by a scholarly interest in marine history. However, there are a few academic institutions, such as Texas A & M, that now have departments specializing in nautical archaeology. As the pages of *Ships and Shipwrecks* demonstrate, archaeology is the most important source of information on early American watercraft, especially smaller ships, which have often been overlooked in historical documentation.

Many of America's early vessels were built by shipwrights who relied on traditional skills, a trained eye, and a knowledge of local waters to design their boats. This was as true for the Mississippi craft of the 1880s as it was for the Inuit kayak. *Ships and Shipwrecks* provides invaluable information, not only about the design and construction of these early ships, but also about the general economic and social conditions of the time. The book pieces together a remarkable story, combining archaeological evidence with historical data supplied by journals, sketches, paintings, and even ethnohistorical accounts. The result is a new perspective on American history.

Bass assembled a team of 12 specialists to tell this story. Margaret Leshikar of Texas A & M describes American indigenous craft, citing myriad sources, ranging from ethnographic data to Maya reliefs. She also emphasizes the important role that the environment has played in shaping watercraft design and maritime adaptation throughout the Americas. Roger C. Smith, of Florida's Division of Historical Resources, takes us on a search for the great explorers' ships and other fifteenth-century wrecks, placing them in their historical context and giving us details about their construction. Donald H. Keith, also of the Institute of Nautical Archaeology, examines two wrecks of the 1554 New Spain fleet off Padre Island, Texas, that yielded a wealth of coins, weapons, and navigational instruments. Incidentally, the Institute of Nautical Archaeology is spearheading a systematic search for discovery-period wrecks in the Caribbean.

Some of the nautical discoveries documented in this book are well known, such as the Basque whalers in Labrador, investigated by Robert Grenier, and the treasure ships of the Spanish Main, which have, unfortunately, inspired the unscrupulous looting of many underwater archaeological sites. The book does venture into less well-charted waters, addressing such subjects as ancient ship design and construction techniques, a discussion led by J. Richard Steffy, another of Bass's colleagues at Texas A & M. Steffy has used the analysis of decaying timbers and metallurgical studies in his reconstruction of ships, such as the colonial vessel *Sea Venture* which sank off Bermuda in 1609. One of Steffy's most impressive achievements was the reconstruction of an early eighteenth-century two-masted river-coaster, recovered from the Black River at Georgetown, South Carolina. This ship carried bulk cargoes between plantations and towns. Steffy's reconstructions of humbler craft have increased our understanding of these vessels, for which there has been virtually no documentation.

The later chapters of *Ships and Shipwrecks* range widely over more recent American history, focusing on gunboats and warships from the French and Indian War on Lake Champlain, the nine ships scuttled by General Cornwallis along the York River in 1781, and the armed sloops *Hamilton* and *Scourge*, which cruised Lake Ontario during the War of 1812, sinking in deep water during a squall. One of the most fascinating chapters describes the diverse steamboats that were popular on inland waterways, in particular the *Bertrand*, a western steamer lost on the Missouri River in 1865, which has been undergoing extensive excavation. Included too are the well-known *Monitor* and the Union gunboat *Cairo* along with the lesser known wrecks of paddle-wheel steamers, blockade runners (see *Archaeology*, September/October 1989), clipper ships, and of course, the *Andrea Doria*.

Ships and Shipwrecks weaves a sophisticated narrative and commemorates the coming of age of nautical archaeology. As the book tells us, the task of chronicling these prosaic chapters of our history has hardly begun. However, the potential is there, the methods are in place, and many wrecks still await discovery: Today's nautical archaeology is nothing less than scientific study carried out underwater rather than on land, offering a unique perspective on life ashore centuries ago. I think that Nathaniel Basse would be proud of his descendant and of the archaeological ties he has developed to his ancestors. ☼

PART III
ISSUES IN CONTEMPORARY
ARCHAEOLOGY

Archaeologists study the material remains of ancient human behavior, using the whole panoply of modern high-technology science to do so. Their fieldwork spans every year of human existence, from our earliest origins to modern times. But all this research revolves around major issues of human history. The articles in Part III discuss current thinking about some of these controversies.

"All About Eve" examines the debate surrounding the origins of anatomically modern humans, *Homo sapiens sapiens*, a debate pitting those who believe we originated in tropical Africa against those who argue for the more-or-less simultaneous evolution of modern people in several parts of the world. Mitochondrial DNA lies at the core of the controversy and is still an immature field of human genetics, but one that promises in coming years to revolutionize our understanding of biological diversity and early population movements. Current archaeological finds favor the African continent as the place where populations of *Homo sapiens sapiens* first evolved out of more archaic forms, between 100,000 and 200,000 years ago. But the fossil evidence is still quite incomplete and the issue still unresolved.

Even more vigorous disagreement surrounds the first settlement of the Americas. Almost everyone agrees that such settlement originated in Siberia, and was at the hands of anatomically modern humans. But when did the first Americans cross the Bering Strait? One school of thought argues for a date in the 40,000-year range, basing its arguments on highly controversial excavations in Brazil. Most scholars believe first settlement took place much later, perhaps at the very end of the Ice Age, and no earlier than 15,000 years ago. Again, the debate is unresolved. "Tracking the First Americans" examines the merits of both cases and analyzes two key excavations, at Meadowcroft Rockshleter in North America and at Boqueirão de Pedra Furada in Brazil. (Since this column was written, new

91

investigations in Brazil have effectively shown the 40,000-year claim for the Brazilian site to be unsupported by the field evidence.)

Modern archaeological excavation is very fine-grained, and works on ever more minute scales. For the first time, archaeologists are looking for the behavior not of groups but of individuals in the past. In particular, they are focusing on the changing roles of men and women in prehistory, using such inconspicuous phenomena as the distribution of artifacts and pathological conditions on womens' joints caused by grinding grain. "A Sexist View of Prehistory" looks at old-fashioned claims of Mother Goddess worship in Europe, the work of archaeologist Marija Gimbutas, who claimed that comparisons between female figures in ancient Europe enabled her to identify a widespread Mother Goddess cult throughout the continent in the fifth millennium B.C. Such claims do not hold up under detailed scientific scrutiny. We compare them to meticulous modern-day researches that use isotope analysis and other approaches to study changing human behavior.

Because the word "cannibalism" raises violent emotions and prejudices, when an expert palaeoanthropologist looks at anthropophagy using well-established methodology for studying animal bones, the results carry great weight. "A Case for Cannibalism" describes the remarkable researches of Tim White on a collection of Anasazi human remains from the American Southwest, which establish baseline criteria for claiming the presence of cannibalism in the archaeological record. White's work sets unassailable standards for scientific verification, but, as he points out, he is nowhere nearer to answering the question as to *why* the Anasazi broke up human bones and presumably consumed their flesh, using bone processing techniques identical to those used on animal remains.

I came across Serge the dog and his travois while paging through the *Plains Anthropologist*, a long established and highly respected regional journal of North American archaeology. Richard Henderson's experiments with replica travois in diverse Plains environments are a classic example of intelligent experimental archaeology. Clearly, precise replication is impossible, but Serge's patient tramps over different kinds of local terrain provide some invaluable insights into the realities of ancient Plains travel. The project also offers a telling reminder of how basic information about even simple prehistoric technology has been lost without trace. And in many cases, too, even the raw materials, like some of those formerly used to make travois, are no longer available or are in short supply.

The last two articles in Part III deal with serious issues confronting modern-day archaeologists: the problem of over-specialization and too narrow training for a rapidly changing discipline, and the scandalous lack of attention paid to final publication of excavations and othr forms of field work. They reflect a time when archaeology is changing from a predominantly academic discipline based at colleges, museums, and universities into a profession concerned with the management of cultural resources and environmental analysis, and also with the enforcement of antiquities and historic preservation legislation. ✺

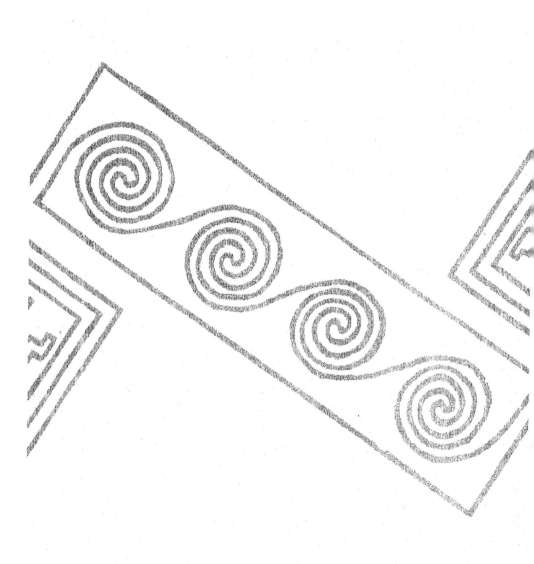

CHAPTER SIXTEEN
ALL ABOUT EVE

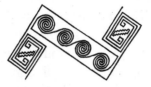

An African Eve is a seductive idea—dark-skinned, strongly built, the primeval woman, mother of us all. But did she actually exist? Was there actually an evolutionary Garden of Eden in Africa where we all originated more than 150,000 years ago?

Some 25 years ago Vincent Sarich of the University of California, Berkeley, used molecular biology to calculate that the ancestors of apes and humans had split from one another between five and seven million years ago—far later than anyone imagined. Sarich's research sparked an interest in molecular clocks, particularly in the mutations of DNA. So-called neutral mutations, which are neither beneficial nor harmful to the survival of the species, accumulate over long periods of time. If this accumulation occurs at a constant rate over time, as most researchers believe, the number of mutations shared by individuals will reflect how closely they are related and can be used to estimate when in the past they shared a common ancestor. Sarich's colleague, the late Alan Wilson, used this approach to reconstruct recent human evolution using DNA from the mitochondria, the energy-producing part of a cell. Wilson described mitochondrial DNA as a "fast-clicking clock," because it accumulates neutral mutations rapidly; making it an ideal tool for studying genetic relationships in modern humans. Mitochondrial DNA is inheirited from the mother alone, and studies based on it trace recent human evolution through the female line. Thus all human mitochondrial DNA must have derived from a common female ancestor. Unlike the biblical Eve, she was not the only woman in her generation. Her mitochondrial DNA, however, was the only line to survive.

Using mitochondrial DNA to study the maternal lineages of living people from around the world, Wilson and others reconstructed ever more refined human family trees. Based on a study of mitochondrial DNA from 147 individuals, they claimed in 1989 that all modern humanity originated in Africa about 200,000 years ago, later migrating to Europe and Asia. Subsequently, Linda Vigilant of Pennsylvania State University refined these results by studying 120 Africans (only 2 Africans and 18 African-Americans had been studied originally). With this new data she traced, and statistically tested, a genealogical tree for *Homo sapiens* that has 15 branches. The 14 deepest branches led only to Africans while the last branch leads to both additional African and to all non-African lineages.

The new "Out-of-Africa" hypothesis caused a sensation. For years, the fossil record for early *Homo sapiens* had been one of the "black holes" of human evolution. There were only a few specimens, mainly from African sites including Border Cave and Klasies River Cave in South Africa, and Omo in Ethiopia at the other end of the continent. Small skull and jaw fragments from these sites displayed surprisingly modern features, yet they were unearthed in archaeological deposits at least 100,000 years old. This was much too early for scientists accustomed to thinking of modern humans as little more than 40,000 years old.

As so often happens, the media soon made the Out-of-Africa theory the scientific flavor of the month. But a vociferous minority, headed by paleontologists Milford Wolpoff and Alan Thorne, oppose it passionately. Wolpoff, who has examined practically every fossil human specimen in existence with meticulous care, has constructed a "regional hypothesis" from the fossil evidence that is diametrically opposed to the Out-of-Africa theory. According to Wolpoff, there was only one population movement out of Africa, archaic *Homo erectus* spreading into Europe and Asia about 1.8 million years ago. Thereafter, modern humans evolved independently in several areas. This, Thorne and Wolpoff say, is "like several individuals paddling in separate corners of a pool: although they maintain their individuality over time, they influence one another with the ripples they raise, which are the equivalent of genes flowing between populations." They believe mitochondrial DNA is useful for "guiding the development of theories," but that fossils are the only basis for confirming them.

The validity of Thorne and Wolpoff's hypothesis depends on finding evidence of anatomical continuity between ancient and more modern human fossils within regions such as Europe and Asia. Citing fossils from early Chinese finds to the robust, archaic-looking ones found at the 35,000-year-old Kow Swamp site in Australia, they claim there is evidence for a stable human morphology over more than 700,000 years in Asia. By 100,000 years ago, according to Thorne and Wolpoff, Asians had developed brain sizes in the modern range, while retaining many archaic characteristics.

As further evidence against the Out-of-Africa theory, Wolpoff and his colleagues state that there are no signs, either in Europe or in Asia, of the sudden arrival of modern humans from outside who replaced existing archaic populations. They also point out, correctly, that the fossil evidence for modern human origins in Africa is, at best, fragmentary.

The debate over Eve, however, has now blossomed in the public arena. A minor furor erupted some months ago when Washington University geneticist Alan Templeton pointed out damaging flaws in the computer analysis used to test the original mitochondrial family tree. "Templeton's pulled the plug on the whole thing," proclaimed Wolpoff with glee in *The New York Times*. While conceding that there were flaws in their statistical arguments, the geneticists say the evidence is overwhelming and that they are working on new ways of generating human family trees. "Overblown," was Linda Vigilant's characterization of the Templeton criticisms.

Are we to believe the molecular biologists, when they argue that mitochondrial DNA tells us things about human evolution that we can never know from fossils alone? Or are we to accept Wolpoff and Thorne's contention that fossils alone are the key? I suspect that the biologists rather than the fossil experts are right, simply because their research tools are so powerful. By comparison, a recent, much ballyhooed fossil discovery from China highlights some of the dangers of working with bones alone. Chinese scholar Li Tianyuan and Dennis Etler of the University of California, Berkeley, described two ancient skulls from China's Hebei Province. The two relatively complete brain cases come from deposits estimated on the basis of nearby fossil animal bones to date to about 350,000 years ago. Li and Etler say the skulls display many archaic features, like long, low cranial vaults. But there are, they claim, many modern features, too, such as rather flat faces and angled cheekbones. They believe the Hebei specimens are transitional between *Homo erectus* and *Homo sapiens*. If this is the case, the fossils support Thorne and Wolpoff's multiregional hypothesis. But this liberal interpretation of two fragmentary skulls is fraught with difficulties. First, the present dating of the Hebei finds is, at best, a good-faith estimate.

Second, Western scholars, who have examined photographs of the specimens, point out that the skulls are much distorted and still encrusted in rocky matrix. Etler admitted to *The New York Times* that the bones were too distorted for accurate measurement, but that the "general forms are suggestive."

Therein lies the crux of the problem. Even when securely dated and well-preserved, the interpretation of minute anatomical features on fossil bones is often controversial. The pace of discovery is slow, the finds are tantalizingly incomplete. There is a temptation to do what Li and Etler have done—to claim evidence for anatomical modernity on the basis of initial impressions. There is a tendency, too, to find what one is looking for—as seems to be the case with the Hebei skulls. Such hasty claims undermine the credibility of the regionalists.

It is likely that neither of today's somewhat simplistic theories will prove to be correct. As research methods will improve and more fossils come to light, the final truth will emerge. We archaeologists should consider ourselves lucky that the molecular biologists are developing research tools that, when more refined, will undoubtedly revolutionize out perceptions not only of our origins but of our biological diversity. More accurate perceptions of these are essential, for the popular understandings of human diversity are still naive, ill-informed, and often downright wrong. And, believe it or not, in this day and age there are still some people who are profoundly bothered by the notion that they may be descended, ultimately, from a dark-skinned, well-muscled African woman, however theoretical she may be. And that is absurd. ☼

CHAPTER SEVENTEEN
TRACKING THE FIRST AMERICANS

"Ancient Find, But How Ancient?" . . . The headline in *The New York Times* for April 17, 1990 stood out from a mass of political news. Correspondent James Brooke had traveled deep into northeastern Brazil in search of the first Americans. He had found them at the Boqueirão de Pedra Furada, deep in the arid São Raimundo Nonato region. Here French archaeologist Nième Guidon and Italian colleague Fabio Parenti were digging in a remote area famous for its fine rock paintings and prolonged human settlement.

Pedra Furada is a deep rockshelter, with fill more than 55 feet in depth. Like other archaeological sites in the São Raimundo Nonato, the shelter contains abundant, and undoubted, evidence of human occupation as far back as about 10,000 years ago. But Guidon and Parenti claim that this remote shelter was occupied much earlier in prehistory, as early as 47,000 years ago. That is a staggeringly early date for human settlement in the Americas, more than 30,000 years earlier than the 15,000-year-old date that represents conventional archaeological wisdom. If the new date is correct, then human beings were living in the New World at a time when Neanderthals flourished in Europe.

Boqueirão de Pedra Furada first made headlines in the British scientific journal *Nature* in 1986. Guidon and her colleagues then claimed they had found 32,000-year-old hearths and stone artifacts in the depths of the Furada. Not only that, they wrote of painted rock fragments going back to at least 17,000 years ago, some of the earliest cave art in the world. The 32,000-year date caused considerable surprise. It was very early, but not impossible, if the evidence for it was adequately documented.

Now Guidon and Parenti have raised the stakes dramatically. They claim to have 21 radiocarbon and thermoluminescence dates associated with human occupation that go back from 14,300 years ago to 47,000 years ago. The two excavators also report that they have discovered charcoal and burned rocks arranged in hearths going back more than 30,000 years in an "unbroken sequence," to quote the *Times*. The 47,000-year date, according to the two, is associated with an ash-filled hearth ringed with a circle of stones.

What are we to make of such claims? Are they based on meticulously collected archaeological data and careful analyses of cave strata, designed to identify and eliminate all possible sources of nonhuman formation of "artifacts" and "hearths"? Or have the excavators been carried away by their discoveries, by the quest for that holiest of archaeological Holy Grails—the very first Native Americans?

I have a horrible feeling that for Pedra Furada the latter is the case. Even after eight years researching and writing about the settlement of the New World, I continue to be amazed at the passions that the debates over the first Americans raise in the archaeological breast. It is as if there is a competition to find the earliest, to break new ground, a competition where specious claims are more important than solid, indisputable archaeological evidence. The recent *Times* story does not help. It carries not only the 47,000-year claim, but also quotes two well-known scholars. One describes the site as "hot stuff," while the other argues that Guidon's early date has been pretty well "deep-sixed" by scholars working in the field. Strong stuff, but anyone who follows the subject soon becomes inured to claims and counterclaims. Ever since I wrote *The Great Journey*, a book about the people of the Americas, a torrent of correspondence has crossed my desk. Many letter writers want me to take sides, to state that I either support the notion of 30,000- or 40,000-year-old settlements in the Americas, or that I join the "diehards" who believe no one ventured into this part of the world until after the Ice Age, some 12,000 years ago. Which side am I on, they want to know. The story in the *Times* is clearly written with side-taking in mind.

What absolute nonsense this is, and how counterproductive for archaeology. The debate over who first settled the Americas and when is important, but it should be entered into with great care. To do otherwise is to demean archaeology as a serious science.

I then recalled a report in the April 1990 issue of *American Antiquity* detailing how archaeology at early sites *should* be conducted. In it, James Adovasio, now director of the Archaeological Institute at Mercyhurst College, and two colleagues summarize a decade of chronological work at the once controversial Meadowcroft Rockshelter, 30 miles southwest of Pittsburgh. Throughout the 1970s, Adovasio and a multidisciplinary research team searched the deep deposits of Meadowcroft with a fine-toothed archaeological comb. Adovasio excavated the intricate layers of the rockshelter, passing through no fewer than 11 strata. With comprehensive dating, he was able to document a remarkable continuity of human occu-pation from about 700 to 12,000 years ago—and considerably earlier. Initial radiocarbon dates from the earliest levels suggested that humans might have occupied the site as early as 19,500 years ago, a little less than 30,000 years after the alleged settlement in northeastern Brazil.

While everyone accepted the chronology for the later levels at Mead-owcroft, many experts were worried by the possibility of contamination in the lowermost levels, either as a result of coal particles in the deposits or through human disturbance. The *American Antiquity* essay is a carefully reasoned analysis of the controversy and a line-by-line response to critics' concerns. Adovasio describes how all possible sources of contamination were removed from the radiocarbon samples and how a new accelerator method was used to check the accuracy of dates determined by other methods.

The Adovasio essay is a model of just how a controversial dating question should be handled. The tone is sober, the data comprehensive, the statistical arguments telling. We can be confident that the question of the age of this most important North American site is as settled as it ever will be. As Adovasio remarks, "it is important to note that the earliest Mead-owcroft dates that have extensive artifactual associations do not argue for any radical extension of the 15,000-year baseline. Perhaps, humans were at Meadowcroft some 2,000 to 3,000 years earlier than the first, well-documented appearance of Clovis people about 11,500 years ago in much of the Americas."

There is a lesson in all this. Adovasio's chronology was questioned by other scientists not on the grounds that it was wrong, but because they were concerned that there might be undetected contamination in the samples.

Over periods of years, Adovasio investigated this possibility with great thoroughness, confirmed the basic validity of his dates, and produced as refined a chronology as he could. Now, he says, it is time to "address the issue of other potential Meadowcrofts." He is correct, but there is definitely a right and a wrong way to do it.

Meadowcroft is a long-term project that has cost tens of thousands of dollars and engaged the best efforts of a talented research team for a decade. A great deal of effort has gone not only into documenting and publishing the finds from the shelter, but also into understanding the complicated sequence of geological and climatic events that contributed to the formation of the occupation deposits at Meadowcroft. In short, we know as well as we ever will how the early deposits were formed and how old they are. Have Guidon and her colleagues worked with the same scientific meticulousness?

Guidon and Parenti's claims fly not only in the face of established chronologies, but in that of scientific archaeology as well. For a start, many archaeologists are deeply suspicious of the Brazilian site. They argue that the hearths were the result of natural forest fires, that runoff in the vicinity of the rockshelter caused mixing in the deposits, that the quartzite "artifacts" from the site result from rockfalls from the cliffs above. How can one make such judgments without seeing the place first hand, the excavators argue? As for the artifacts, Parenti says he is certain of at least 200 or 300 of the artifacts. According to the *Times*, he implies he is more qualified to make that judgment than his critics are because he is more accustomed than American archaeologists to examining the kinds of primitive artifacts found with people who lived more than 40,000 years ago. This is hardly a reasoned and sober response to legitimate scientific objections.

Few American scholars have visited São Raimundo Nonato, which is far from the beaten track. This means that Guidon and her team of excavators have been working in much greater isolation than James Adovasio did at Meadowcroft. Dozens of scholars visited his excavation, to the great intellectual benefit of all concerned. Apart from inevitable language barriers, those who labor at Pedra Furada have few first-hand opportunities to discuss with other experts their stratigraphic and geological observations, or their claims for hearths and early stone tools.

In their eagerness to defend their cherished claims, the excavators of Boqueirão de Pedra Furada have missed the real point that their critics are trying to make. These experts are not necessarily saying that Guidon is wrong, nor are they taking sides. What, they ask, is the *basis* for the claim for a 47,000-year-old settlement in the Americas other than simple observation and instinct? For instance, how did the deposits in which the hearth and its stones were discovered form? How did the ash concentration accumulate? As a result of natural fires, or through deliberate human action? Have flakes from the early levels been fitted together to reconstruct flaking practices and stone technology? What possible natural causes for flaking quartzite could account for the "tools," if any? To date, it is fair to say that we have only ever-earlier datings and flat claims to work with. Judging from the available literature and conversations with many of my colleagues, these claims are based on the notion of "I observed this; trust my observations." The careful work at Meadowcroft has set a standard; personal conviction is no longer sufficient.

What is needed at Boqueirão de Pedra Furada is another Meadowcroft project, where every possibility is exhaustively and laboriously worked through. Putting it bluntly, a claim for 47,000-year-old human settlement in the Americas has to be documented beyond a reasonable doubt by methods that use modern science to eliminate the possibilities that the "hearths" and "stone tools" were created by natural phenomena. Any other approach is intellectually and archaeologically bankrupt. ❀

CHAPTER EIGHTEEN

A SEXIST VIEW
OF PREHISTORY

F ads and fancies come and go not only among the general public but within the academic community as well. One of the latest of these fads, popular with some feminist scholars and New Age groupies, is the cult of the Mother Goddess.

Marija Gimbutas of the University of California at Los Angeles is a principal advocate for this cult, having worked at Neolithic and Bronze Age sites in central Europe for decades. She has long had a preoccupation with Mother Goddesses in what she calls "Old Europe," and writes in her latest book, *The Civilization of the Goddess*: "According to myriad images that have survived from the great span of European prehistory on the Eurasian continents, it was the sovereign mystery and creative power of the female as the source of life that developed into the earliest religious experiences." And, says Gimbutas, the great Mother Goddess became the "cosmic giver and taker of life, ever able to renew Herself within the eternal cycle of birth, death, and rebirth."

Gimbutas traces the beginnings of this primordial cult back more than 20,000 years. The Mother Goddess, she says, came into her own during an explosion of artistic creativity in the late Ice Age. Artists depicted animals and symbols in which modern scholars have been able to discern "an iconography of the Goddess," comprising "several kinds of abstract and hieroglyphic symbols." And, she contends, these symbols persisted into Neolithic times (6500–3500 B.C.). According to Gimbutas, this period saw a great flowering of the Mother Goddess cult and an era of agricultural prosperity within a peace-loving, egalitarian matrilineal society, which began in the Aegean, central Balkans, and Adriatic regions and quickly spread to what is now Eastern Europe. Unfortunately, writes Gimbutas, this prehistoric Garden of Eden came to an end in the mid-fourth millennium B.C. when a warlike, patriarchal culture from the Black Sea displaced the placid peoples of "Old Europe."

Reading her latest book on the Mother Goddess, I felt like a disciple being led back into the past by a prophetess who held the key to the Sacred Mysteries. We pass from site to site, from image to image, from the Old Stone Age to modern Czechoslovakia, with effortless ease, following symbols of the Mother Goddess through the millennia. It is all so simple, so enlightening.

But, I doubt if Marija Gimbutas has many followers among her archaeological colleagues, for the way in which she threads together her goddess story involves the most subjective of judgments at every stage. How can one possibly trace intangible religious beliefs from 18,000 to 8,000 years ago purely on what are claimed to be resemblances in artistic motifs? Yet Gimbutas strings together stylistic motifs from different periods of prehistory, motifs so simple they occur in art from many parts of the world. This form of analysis stretches scientific credibility beyond reasonable bounds.

Gimbutas places women and their fecundity at the heart of prehistoric life, and writes as if the goddess is a matter of scientific certainty. Few archaeologists would disagree that fertility rituals were of vital importance in prehistoric life for tens of thousands of years, as they are in many societies today. But to accept the probable existence of such rituals is very different from claiming that there was a primordial Mother Goddess, with a capital M and G, who presided for millennia over what a *New York Times* reviewer called a "paradise lost." Putting it bluntly, Gimbutas's Mother Goddess thesis does not reflect the incredible complexity of what we now know about hunter-gatherer and farming societies in prehistoric Europe. The 529 pages of *Civilization* are crammed with descriptions and interpretations of figurines and art motifs, shrines and dwellings, that are remarkable for their uncritical subjectivity. A typical example: "More than half the figurines of Old Europe appear to be nude above the hips, hence we presume they represent goddesses or priestesses as they enact rituals." The entire panoply of the Mother Goddess thesis is based on such presumptions rather than on critical, contextual analysis.

The study of gender has come late to archaeology, and there are few studies for researchers in other fields to turn to. Gimbutas's sweeping generalizations appeal to feminist scholars engaged in studies of patriarchal institutions in Christianity and Judaism. The close relationships among fertility, motherhood, and Earth invoked by the Mother Goddess cult are of fundamental interest to an emerging school of ecofeminists studying women's roles in ecological and environmental issues.

While Gimbutas's work is sometimes hailed as pioneering research into the role of women in prehistory, nothing could be further from the truth. In fact, she projects a Eurocentric and frankly sexist view of prehistory, which is remarkable for its subjective generalizations and outdated research methods. Her image of Old Europe is uncannily similar to that of the Noble Savage so popular with nineteenth-century romantic novelists. Such simplistic perspectives have a deep popular appeal in a world where science and, for that matter, archaeology are becoming ever more complex. Whatever its superficial appeal, the Mother Goddess theory is not science but speculation.

While I was reading *The Civilization of the Goddess*, I chanced upon archaeologist Christine Hastorf's remarkable study of Andean men and women in Prehispanic Sausa society. The Sausa were maize and potato farmers who lived in highland Peru's northern Mantaro Valley. Before the Inka took control, in about A.D. 1460, the Sausa lived in local population groups of several thousand people. Their conquerors, anxious to increase maize production, dispersed them into small village settlements. Hastorf was interested in the role of women resulting from the Inka conquest. She approached this fundamental question not by marshaling subjective evidence but by examining the changing distribution of food remains in excavated settlements, and changing dietary evidence obtained by isotope analyses of skeletons from ancient Sausa villages.

As they have been for centuries in Andean households, women are responsible for food preparation and storage. Hastorf, an expert on native plants, believes that there is a relationship between the distribution of plant remains in Sausa dwellings and compounds and the activities of men and women. In households with male heads, for example, she found the most diverse plant remains in kitchen areas, and fewer types elsewhere in the compound where other activities took place. Households with a female head had concentrations of plant remains not only in the kitchen area but on the patio, as if different rules on the preparation of food and its consumption were followed.

Hastorf then plotted the distribution of crop seeds in pre-Inka structures, which date to a time when maize was less common, and found that the inhabitants of every dwelling used and consumed a wide range of plant foods, especially potatoes and legumes. Maize occurred mostly in patio areas. It was here, argues Hastorf, that such communal activities as the making of corn-based beer took place—the beer being a commodity that was a vital part of ritual, social, and political meetings. A later, Inka-period compound yielded fewer potatoes and much more maize. Here the processing of corn was more concentrated, with little burning of corn, as if more of it were consumed as beer. Hastorf believes the dense and restricted distribution of maize in the later compound might reflect more intensified processing of corn by women. Inka policies that sought a constant rise in maize production, regular taxation in the form of labor and produce, led to more restrictive roles for women—roles that supported male activities.

Hastorf then turned to the skeletons found in the compounds, studying the stable carbon isotopes in bone collagen extracted from them. She found pre-Inka diets were the same for men and women, mainly quinoa and tubers, with some maize. This suggests that if corn-based beer were being consumed, it was shared between men and women. The skeletons that postdated the Inka conquest revealed a higher consumption of maize, but half of the male diets were much richer in maize than that of the women. Hastorf believes this reflects changed social conditions under Inka rule. The women were processing much more maize into beer, which was consumed not by everyone but by a relatively small proportion of the males in the community. Furthermore, most men were eating more meat than women. The dietary differences reflect a changed political climate, in which the Sausa, once small groups, were now incorporated into a larger sphere that depended on men becoming involved in far more gatherings, rituals, and obligatory tasks during which beer was consumed. The women worked harder, but their position outside the home was more restricted under the Inka regime.

The Sausa example shows how archaeological data, meticulously gathered from many sources, can document the change in men's and women's roles in a given society. In addition to archaeological evidence, Hastorf had the advantage of working with rich ethnographic and historical sources. While these are, of course, lacking for the Stone Age, the lesson is clear. Gender relations have always been dynamic and can hardly be inferred from simple decorative motifs on pots or figurines.

Hastorf shows us a plausible and fascinating road ahead. This kind of research is a far cry from sweeping generalizations about Mother Goddesses and fertility cults. For me, Hastorf's innovative approach to gender and the role of women in prehistory is far more intriguing. ✺

CHAPTER NINETEEN
A CASE FOR CANNIBALISM

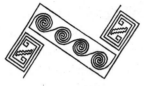

People dining on other people? The image fascinates and repels. Historian William Prescott was so moved by Spanish accounts of Aztec human culinary fare that he wrote of "a banquet teeming with delicious beverages and delicate viands, prepared with art and attended by both sexes." As archaeologists have found, it's easy to accuse our ancestors of cannibalism, but extremely hard to prove it. Mark Twain remarked more than a century ago, "paleontology holds a coroner's inquest . . . on an unpleasantness which transpired in the quaternary, and calmly lays it on MAN, and then adds to it what purports to be evidence of CANNIBAL-ISM." Victorian science often painted our ancestors as brutish, violent folk, who shopped their cemeteries for food. "Does this not look like taking advantage of a gentleman who has been dead for two million years?" Twain remarked cynically. Proof of cannibalism is as elusive today as it was to the Victorians.

Passions apart, cannibalism, or anthropophagy, remains an enigma in human history. After all, this is hardly a subject that can be studied with the classic anthropological technique of participant observation. There remain, however, the dispassionate eyes of archaeology and biological anthropology. One of the strengths of our discipline is that artifacts do not lie, making palaeoanthropologist Tim White's exhaustive analysis of 2,106 human bone fragments from an obscure Anasazi pueblo site in Mancos Canyon, Colorado, of remarkable importance.

The evidence suggests that just after A.D. 1100, two to six families lived in an L-shaped pueblo overlooking the Mancos River. A half century later, the pueblo was torn down and another erected in its place. Archaeologist Larry Nordby excavated the second pueblo in 1973, recovering a number of burials, but also a series of "bone beds"—unarticulated and highly fragmentary human bones—from the earlier pueblo. Even superficial examination showed they had been broken before being dumped like discarded food remains. Here was an unusual chance to study the osteology of cannibalism.

It took White and his colleagues five years to study the 2,106 fragments. Forensic analyses of this kind resemble those conducted during a murder investigation. One looks for evidence of traumatic injuries that might have been the cause of death. Cannibalism adds another dimension—how the human remains were processed. If the Mancos dead had been chopped up for meat, one might reasonably expect those who butchered them to use the same methods they would employ on other mammals—skin the carcass, then dismember it before defleshing the bones and breaking them to extract the marrow. White refitted as many of the bones as possible, a time-consuming job that enabled him to examine larger areas of surface damage. He was also able to determine that the remains were from 29 individuals, 17 of them young adults, the rest children. The teeth showed signs of dental hypoplasia—checks in growth resulting from nutritional stress and dietary inadequacies—and the bones exhibited porotic hyperostosis, caused by certain anemias and infectious diseases. Next, he turned to the surface markings on the bones. He examined each fragment at low magnification under harsh, incandescent light, which revealed tiny cutmarks, traces of burning or hitting, and other topographic details. Many limb-bone shaft and rib fragments were both polished and abraded at each end. At first, White theorized these bones had been used as tools. But when he examined the animal bone fragments from other Southwestern sites, he discovered a pattern, as if hundreds of bones had been similarly modified. He broke some fresh mule deer limb bones into splinters and articular ends with a stone hammer, put 18 on one side as control specimens, then boiled the remainder for three hours in a replica of an Anasazi cooking pot. Once the water had cooled, he scraped away a ring of fat from the sides of the vessel with one fragment, then examined the other bones with the naked eye and under a 10-power hand lens. In many cases, the ends of the bone splinters displayed beveling and rounding, exactly like those on the human bones from Mancos. As bone ends come into contact with the pot walls, they became worn; the turbulence causes faceting and sometimes polishing of the fragment. When White examined the bones under magnification, tiny scratch marks showed up under the oblique light, marks made by

110

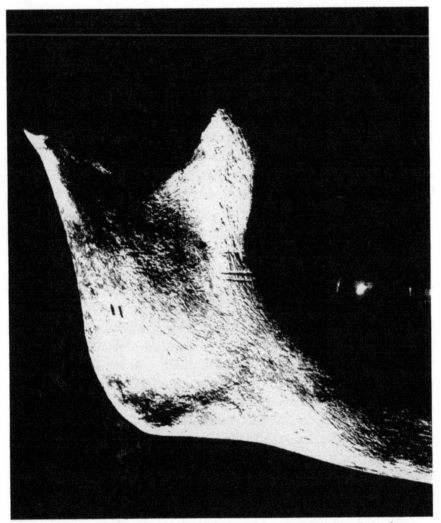

Evidence for processing of human flesh. Cut-marks on an Anasazi jaw bone from Mancos Canyon, Colorado. Photograph by T. White. Reprinted with permission.

individual grains of rock-grit temper used by the pot maker to bind the clay together. The bone fragment used to scrape the fat away from the walls of the pot displayed abrasion and polish, as well as distinctive striations perpendicular to the axis of the scraping edge. White identified a bone splinter from Mancos that had been similarly used. Almost certainly, then, the people who broke up the human bones at Mancos cooked at least some of them in clay vessels and scraped the fat off the ceramic surface.

White also found that 87 percent of the 2,106 bones had been fractured at about the time of death. Distinctive conchoidal scars tell of sharp objects being used to open skull vaults to get at the nutritious brain tissue. He discovered that, with the exception of some neck vertebrae, most vertebrae spines and arches had been detached. The butchers had removed ribs from the body by levering them against the backbone. Then they had broken individual ribs into smaller portions. Hammerstones had been used to break larger limb bones from which marrow was extracted.

Tim White's Mancos work involves meticulous study of bone damage, not speculation, to identify cannibalism. Using White's exacting criteria we may actually underestimate the prevalence of cannibalism in the past. But it is one thing to document butchery of human remains, quite another thing to prove cannibalism. White is certain that the Mancos bones were processed for food, for they show no signs of standard dismemberment, as one might expect in mortuary rituals. Significantly, the jaw and facial bones, among the most delicate in the entire skeleton, are often relatively intact, whereas other bones were reduced literally to powder. Fracturing and destruction were limited to those bones with the most nutritional value.

Why did the Anasazi at Mancos engage in cannibalism? Out of desperate necessity, or because of ceremonies connected with warfare? The violence used to break up the Mancos bones resulted not from hand-to-hand violence, but from butchery processes like those routinely used on animals. The Anasazi and other Southwestern groups certainly fought one another, for remains of war casualites have been identified at several sites. At Mancos, warfare may have caused the death of people who were then butchered for food, but there is no way of proving this. Perhaps famine was a factor. Every Anasazi pueblo was at the mercy of the harsh, unpredictable climate of the Colorado Plateau. Even a minor shift in rainfall patterns could bring hunger, for there were few wild plant foods to fall back on in lean times. The people responded to uncertainty by storing foods, by diversifying their diet, by trading, and by cultivating social relationships with their neighbors. But still the lean years came. Pioneer anthropologist Frank Cushing, who lived among the Zuni in the 1870s, recorded legends of a memorable Southwestern famine: "At last the corn was all gone. The people were pitiably poor. They were so weak that they could not hunt through the snow, therefore a great famine spread through the village. At last the people were compelled to gather old bones and grind them for meal." To the Mancos Anasazi, the nutrition in the human body may have meant the difference between life and death. Unfortunately, human bones never bear telltale marks of starvation, even though they may reveal signs of long-term nutritional stress.

Tim White has documented cannibalism at Mancos with impressive thoroughness, but he is no closer to explaining why it took place than his predecessors. Therein lies the great frustration of archaeology—one can rarely hear the voices of those whose acts are preserved in the archaeological record, even if one can document beyond all scientific doubt that they ate one another. ❁

CHAPTER TWENTY
TEACHING NEW DOGS OLD TRICKS

I've watched scientists "fight" one another with replicated Bronze Age swords, make perfect Clovis points, and blow ancient Egyptian trumpets. All this is fascinating, so when I saw Richard Henderson's article about experiments with the travois in the *Plains Anthropologist*, my pulse quickened. I'd read about the travois, the dog-drawn sled used by the Plains Indians, but I had never met anyone who had seen one in operation. I'd always wondered, for example, how people killing hundreds of bison in mass stampedes transported all the meat they butchered and dried. At the Olsen Chubbock site in Colorado, for instance, Paeo-Indian hunters drove a herd of about 150 bison into a narrow arroyo about 6500 B.C. Joe Ben Wheat, who excavated the site in 1958, estimated that the hunters butchered about 75 percent of the kill, taking the hides and more than 64,000 pounds of meat, fat, and edible internal organs. But how did they move this bounty? Wheat theorized they used the travois. Consulting historical accounts, he concluded that an average travois load amounted to about 50 pounds.

When Henderson, an archaeologist at the University of East Anglia, decided to replicate travois travel, he turned to the account of Buffalo-bird Woman, a Hidatsa Indian from the Missouri Valley, recorded by anthropologist Gilbert Wilson in 1924. Following her description, Henderson built his replica using light and flexible aspen for poles. The travois consisted of two straight poles that were lashed together at their thinner ends with sinew to form an A-frame about eight feet, three inches long and about three feet, nine inches across at the base. While the broad ends of the poles dragged on the ground, the point of the A met and crossed over the small of the dog's back, the ends of the poles extending above the ears. To prevent the dog's back from chafing, bison hide was used to cover the top of the

114

frame. The load was placed either on a wooden hoop made of bent willow and thongs or simple wood pieces that were attached to the frame poles. The dog pulled the travois from the chest, straining against a wide, horizontal chest strap essentially the same as those used by modern dog sledders. Henderson copied the 1924 specifications, but at a slightly reduced size (92 percent), to accommodate a somewhat smaller modern dog. He substituted synthetic for animal sinew lashing and made the chest belt of cow skin instead of buffalo hide.

Finding a suitable dog proved a challenge since Plains dogs are extinct. The celebrated fur trader Alexander Ross observed in the 1820s that Indian dogs near Fort Edmonton were "in general of the wolf-breed, and are said to be vigorous and long winded: a hundred miles a day is a common journey for them." Henderson chose an Alaskan husky as a modern substitute, a non-purebred selected for endurance and pulling abilities over many generations. Alaskan huskies date back to the Alaskan and Klondike gold rushes, and are a mix of imported animals and hardy northern forms like Siberian huskies and Eskimo dogs. The Alaskan husky has all the qualities of the Plains dog, but its fur is much longer. It is also longer-legged, adapted to pulling light sleds at high speeds. Henderson looked for a short-haired, short-distance husky trained for running longer, slower races over many days. He found a Saskatchewan sled-dog handler with just the right dog, an eight-year-old named Serge.

A highly intelligent lead dog, Serge was trained from a puppy to haul loads. Armed with Serge and his travois, Henderson set out to replicate travois travel. All he had to go on were travelers' and Indians' estimates of loads and distances. In 1924, Wolf-Chief, also a Hidatsa, told Gilbert Wilson that a load of 80 to 100 pounds would travel about seven miles in three to four hours. The Austrian explorer Prinz von Maximillian, who traveled widely on the Plains in 1833, noted that dogs could travel 30 miles, rest for one hour, then journey farther. Henderson found a consensus among the early accounts that dogs traveled easier and farther during the winter when their paws padded over the crusty snow. In the summer the dogs needed a great deal of water.

Henderson took Serge on long- and short-haul trips over varied terrain in the Qu'Appelle Valley of Saskatchewan and Manitoba and on adjacent plains. On their journeys, Serge followed Henderson. This allowed the dog to pick a route for himself, an advantage when a 30-pound load forced Serge to zigzag his way up steep slopes. He had to do the same downhill, otherwise the travois would slide forward over his head. Nor was maneuvering easy; the dog required a 16-foot turning radius. Backing up was impossible. On occasion, Serge yielded to temptation and plunged into thick brush in pursuit of a deer. He could travel comfortably through scrub about three feet high, but the travois had to be carried through narrow gullies. The dog balked at water; Henderson had to carry everything across the Qu'Appelle River, including the reluctant Serge. In historic times, the Hidatsa held the dragging end out of the water, while the harnessed dog swam across, but Serge had a common husky phobia of water. On occasional patches of native prairie, the thick mat of dried grass cushioned the dog's feet and the poles glided across the ground as easily as over snow. Throughout the trials, man and dog traveled at a slow walking pace of less than two miles an hour.

Serge could pull about 46 pounds in the fall, but only 30 in the summer. During the hot months, Henderson walked as far as possible during the morning hours, before the heat affected the dog's performance. Since midsummer temperatures in Plains Saskatchewan reach the 80s, a travel time of four to five hours was the most one could expect. In short-distance trials Serge hauled a load of 50 pounds over a 1.25-mile-long grassland test course. Henderson theorizes the dog could have carried 60 pounds over short distances with ease, but that such a load was about the upper limit. Henderson makes a distinction between short-load carrying journeys to fetch firewood or bring meat back to camp, which were feasible in the summer, and long seasonal camp moves, where loads would be much lighter. As much as 100 pounds or so may have been dragged by larger dogs on short trips. For long trips, under ideal circumstances, a full day of travel with travois loads in the 50-pound range at speeds of about two or three miles an hour would have been entirely feasible. Serge, the hero of the investigation, proved that Joe Ben Wheat's original estimate of what a dog could pull was not far out of line. ☀

CHAPTER TWENTY-ONE
THE ARROGANT ARCHAEOLOGIST

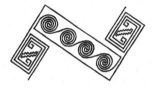

For a moment I saw red, felt sheer blinding fury. Controlling myself with an effort, I gazed in disgust and horror at the ravaged shell midden. I was hiking for pleasure along the southern California coast and looting was far from my mind. Memories of the Slack Farm affair came vividly to mind, that notorious looting event that left a late prehistoric site in Kentucky looking like a scarred battleground (see Chapter 23, "Black Day at Slack Farm"). Every time I come across instances of pothunting, I find them harder to rationalize, and even harder to understand. Why do people do this? For money? To satisfy a lust to own a piece of the past? Is it sheer ignorance about archaeology and the importance of the past? Or are they seeking to emulate the fictional adventures of Indiana Jones? What makes me even madder is that few people seem to care that the past is vanishing before our eyes. Many of my nonprofessional friends just shrug and change the subject. You cannot entirely blame them: most would not know an archaeological site if it was right under their feet. Even worse, some of my archaeological friends just shrug, and that's what makes me maddest of all.

John Neary ("Project Sting," *Archaeology*, September/October 1993) tells us that recent undercover operations have put a chill on some collecting activity in the Southwest. Clearly, these tactics, expensive as they are, work well and should be expanded. Looting statistics are daunting. According to Sherry Hunt, Elwood Jones, and Martin McAllister, authors of *Archaeological Resource Protection* (Washington, DC: Preservation Press, 1992), more than one-third of the known sites in the Four Corners region have been damaged by looters. Of the 1,720 violations reported in Park Service statistics for 1985 through 1987, only about 11 percent resulted in arrests or citations, and there were only 94 convictions.

If there is a solution to the looting problem, it is changing public attitudes toward the collecting of antiquities. This will take years, and will require a full-time commitment by hundreds, if not thousands, of professional archaeologists, not only in this country, but all over the world. It is our responsibility and cannot be left to teachers and bureaucrats. Yet, sadly, in many ways we are the greatest offenders. Our professional organizations condemn looting—they do so in uncompromising terms—but we have not made conservation, ethics, and public education the core of our archaeological enterprise.

Archaeologists live within a hierarchical value system that considers research, excavation, new discoveries, and publication the pinnacle of achievement. Anything else, for all their talk to the contrary, is secondary to these enterprises. Almost all doctoral programs in archaeology emphasize basic research. They produce narrowly focused academic researchers, future generations of professors who will themselves, in turn, train even more specialized archaeologists. The emphasis is often on high-profile research, where the chances of spectacular discoveries are higher than average, the potential for funding is considered promising, and the fieldwork will bring prestige, visibility, and, pinnacle of academic pinnacles, perhaps even a story in *The New York Times*. This is the kind of enterprise beloved of many academic deans and department heads, research that brings luster and financial resources to an institution. I am irresistibly reminded of the expedition mentality that drove so much late nineteenth-century archaeology—the University of Pennsylvania's research at Nippur in Mesopotamia is a classic example. It worked at Nippur, indeed at Ur, in an archaeological world where there were so few professionals. Today, academic archaeology is big business, turning out hundreds of Ph.D. students a year, yet the old mentality and values drive the field. Why do we persist in producing more doctoral students in specialized fields that are already overcrowded when there is so much urgent work to be done on the global threat to the past? I suspect we do because it is, well, sexier to hire a specialist in Oldowan technology or Inka urbanism than in the impact of tourism on the archaeological record.

This same skewed value system pays lip service to teaching, conservation and resource management, and the administering of the archaeological record. But, when push comes to shove, these subjects take a back seat to research. Yes, much academic research is carried out under the rubric of cultural resource management—survey, excavation, and mitigation—aimed at preserving or recording sites before they vanish under bulldozers. But very often academic research, especially excavation, proceeds without consideration of conservation issues or site management whatsoever. In fact, many academics are woefully ignorant of the extent of the damage to the archaeological record, forgetting that their own annual digs are also eroding the same human archives, often at breakneck speed. How many academics pause to think about conserving a site before they dig it? Surprisingly few . . . .

Very few archaeology graduate programs anywhere expose their students to issues of conservation, ethics, and basic archaeological values—unless they are curricula specifically addressing cultural resource management. Out of curiosity, I telephoned a random selection of archaeology graduate advisers at major universities around the country and asked them what ethics and conservation courses were taught to graduate students. Almost invariably, these topics were sidelines. "Oh, we talk about reburial in one lecture," one well-known archaeologist told me in a tired voice. "But it's very political. The Ph.D. is, after all, a research degree." What arrogant nonsense!

The looting problem is not going away. The Park Service alone reports a 40 percent increase in violations over the past few years, and you can be sure that its statistics are just the tip of the iceberg. At the same time, one learns that at least 100 archaeologists with Ph.D.s in Maya archaeology are looking for permanent employment. Unemployed classical archaeologists could almost form a professional society. These people may be excellent scholars, but they are not the kind of archaeologists we need in such large numbers today. We need people who will devote prestigious careers to conservation, to research into the fundamental problems confronting the archaeological record. Without such research, we are, both government and academics, fumbling in the dark.

Basic research is important to the vitality of our discipline. But do we need so many, ever more trivial, studies when fundamental, admittedly less glamorous, issues need our attention? Fascinating opportunities await the ambitious scholar, fundamental research as important, if not more so, than much of the basic inquiry that fills our journals. What is the psychology of collecting? What is it that impels people to transform their fascination with the past into a lust to own it? The last definitive work on this subject was done, I believe, in the 1920s. What do we know about the psychology and culture of professional pot-hunters and looters? Can such research help us develop tactics for combating looting? What about archaeological tourism? What are the effects of tens of thousands of visitors on the rich archaeological record of, say, Britain, Egypt, or Mexico? What strategies are archaeologists developing in collaboration with governments everywhere to minimize the impact on the finite archaeological record? I know of no Ph.D. program in this country that places a high priority on research of this type. Everything is theory, fieldwork, and publication. About the only organization concerned with these issues on a global basis is the Getty Conservation Institute. The Getty's efforts are invaluable, as are those of other international organizations, and of the Archaeological Conservancy closer to home.

I have been told by colleagues that research into such questions is "unimportant" or "marginal." What utter nonsense in this day and age, when the archaeological record evaporates around us daily. Surely we must now take a close look at our own value systems and priorities, at archaeological ethics and curricula. How do we, as professional scholars and practitioners of a noble art, intend to insure its survival for our grandchildren to enjoy?

Yes, this is a column written in the heat of anger, soon after walking over looters' trenches. But this anger will be channeled into a closer look at my own teaching of graduates and undergraduates, and into more columns that look at the ethical issues of archaeology and at conservation. After all, we cannot do much to steer the public's fascination with the past into benign and nondestructive directions unless we clean up our own act. Our own comfortable, sometimes arrogant attitude is much divorced from reality. It is time we took stock. We owe it to our grandchildren, if nothing else. ☀

CHAPTER TWENTY-TWO

ARCHAEOLOGY'S DIRTY SECRET

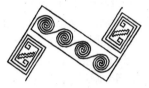

S ome years ago, I attended a retirement party for a distinguished colleague at a prominent midwestern university. Several generations of former students were on hand to praise his many seasons of fieldwork at home and abroad. But they were tactful not to mention one problem with their beloved mentor's career: only one of his excavations had ever been published in full. Alas, the professor has now passed on, leaving behind nothing but sketchy field notes and a museum storeroom full of inadequately labeled artifacts. Even in retirement he could not find the time to publish his fieldwork. In fact he was still digging right up to the end. The loss to science is incalculable.

I was brought up to believe that publishing one's research was a sacred principle of archaeology, a task to be completed before new excavations were begun. The great British Egyptologist Flinders Petrie was an early advocate of prompt and full publication. His reports are verbose and far from complete by modern standards, but at least they provide a body of basic information with which to work. Mortimer Wheeler was also careful to publish his excavations in full. My mentors did not always practice what they preached, but they taught us that prompt and full publication was a fundamental responsibility for any archaeologist who ventures into the field. The archaeological world has changed since Wheeler's day. A generation ago most site reports were the work of a single scholar. Today even a modest dig can involve a team of specialists and a quantity of data that may take years to study and write up. Ironically, in an academic culture that considers publication the most desirable of all scholarly activities, most archaeologists prefer to keep on digging.

The common forum for presenting field data is the academic conference, where 20-minute papers summarize new work. In recent years, publishers have printed volume after volume of such papers, often grouped under a general title, with little editorial coherence. Invariably, conference papers give a nod to current theoretical debates, present some limited original data, and end with a brief synthesis noting how the new work advances research in a particular subject area. Often, the same paper appears in several places, recast slightly to reflect a different audience or academic emphasis. In an academic world where jobs are scarce and publication of any kind is seen as the road to employment, such bibliography-padding has become commonplace, if not endemic. In one's later career the pressure to publish such papers to obtain tenure and regular promotions continues unabated. Too often definitive reports on sites, artifacts, or survey work never appear.

I know of numerous preliminary reports published a generation ago that are still the only source of basic information on excavations of first-rate importance. There are major Lower Paleolithic sites in sub-Saharan Africa excavated in the 1950s and 1960s that are still accessible only from such reports. The same can be said for many important North American and Mesoamerican excavations of the 1970s. Much of the evidence for early agriculture in Europe and the Near East is only available in the periodical literature. Kathleen Kenyon's famous excavations at Jericho are still incompletely published. Some classical excavations have been underway for decades, with no sign that digging will stop and long-term publication begin. Some guilty parties argue that laboratory work must come first and that the whole process takes longer than it did a generation ago. But if you look closely you will find the same people hard at work in the field each year, digging up yet another site.

Clearly an overwhelming case can be made for less excavation and more analysis of previous work. Unfortunately, our scholarly culture rewards people for new and original research, sometimes defined in the narrowest terms as participation in an active fieldwork program. Grant-giving agencies contribute to the problem by funding field research while rarely giving monies for laboratory analysis or publication. Neither is a terribly sexy pursuit in a world in which museums and universities thrive on headline-catching discoveries, and, to quote a recent University of California staff document, "productive faculty publishing in refereed journals." The problem is further compounded by the exigencies of cultural resource management or salvage archaeology, whose requirements for prompt reporting result for the most part in factual accounts with limited, if not restricted, distribution. A researcher can spend days, sometimes months, tracking down what is technically published information. Meanwhile, definitive archaeological monographs, such as those on the Maya city of Tikal that appear at regular intervals, are becoming a rarity. Few outlets remain for such valuable studies. Economic realities make it ever harder for even the best endowed academic presses to produce such monographs.

Surprisingly, there is little, if any, academic discussion of these issues. Perusing the programs of several major conferences, I see no panel sessions on this issue, nor on alternative means of disseminating archaeological data. Hershel Shanks, editor of *Biblical Archaeology Review*, calls the crisis "archaeology's dirty secret." In a recent editorial, he recommended the creation of a new profession: archaeology editor/writer, "specialists who know how to publish reports."

The obligation to publish basic research is a fundamental part of archaeological ethics; some would say it is the most fundamental. It is enshrined in the Archaeological Institute of America's recently adopted Code of Professional Standards: "Archaeologists should make public the results of their research in a timely fashion, making evidence available to others if publication is not accomplished within a reasonable time. All research projects should concern specific plans for conservation, preservation, and publication from the very outset, and funds should be secured for such purposes."

Desktop publishing, CD-ROMs, and other electronic media offer fascinating opportunities for publication, and for distribution of research results and data over the Internet and other such channels. Electronics offer staggering possibilities for wide distribution of highly specialized, peer-reviewed monographs and reports. Soon, researchers will have interactive access to their colleagues' and predecessors' artifact data bases. Such access will make new demands on archaeologists to curate and analyze their data promptly. The demands of the electronic forum will make it harder to duck the responsibility of preparing one's data for scholarly use and scrutiny. In many cases, "publication" will consist of meticulously organized data bases, including graphics. The compiling of such data bases raises fascinating implications for future financing of archaeological projects. Grant-giving agencies will have to bow to the new reality and finance such far-from-spectacular activities, while cutting back on funding for more excavations.

Archaeologists have a clear obligation to publish their research promptly, and in full. After all, ours is the only science that "murders its informants," as American archaeologist Kent Flannery once put it. If we were to devote as much time to publishing as we do to excavating, we would not be accused, with some justification, of being a self-serving, special interest group that keeps its finds to itself. Some of those who make such accusations are now picking up on the publishing problem and arguing that by not producing final reports we are effectively looters ourselves. Writing final reports and monographs is far from glamorous work. But as Mortimer Wheeler and others pointed out many years ago, only the archaeologist who did the work and led the research team can write the final and definitive report that records exactly what was found and what it means. We are witnessing a sea change in the way archaeologists go about business. I do not agree with Hershel Shanks that the solution lies in specialist report writers. It lies in archaeologists living up to their fundamental responsibilities. Fortunately, creative solutions await those bold enough to seize them. ✷

PART IV
ARCHAEOLOGY
AND SOCIETY

Archaeology is unlike almost any other academic discipline except, perhaps, astronomy—in that all its research is carried out under close public scrutiny, and sometimes raises great passion among large numbers of people. The archaeologist is an integral part of the modern world, recognized by everyone as a legitimate scientist, not a mere treasure hunter out for a pharaoh's gold.

Unfortunately, the intense public interest in archaeology sometimes manifests itself in destructive ways. Looters, pothunters, and professional collectors regard archaeological sites as their private game reserve, to be mined haphazardly for fun and profit. In some parts of the United States, notably in the Southwest and Midwest, the looting of archaeological sites on unprotected private lands has reached crisis proportions. "Black Day at Slack Farm" tells the story of one tragic example of looting and illogical destruction, which resulted in the loss of an entire chapter of Native American history. Sadly, the same story is repeated again and again all over the world. The high prices paid for antiquities on the open market make looting a profitable enterprise, even, in some parts of the world, a highly organized industry. There is a real danger that within another century most of the finite archives of the human past will have vanished in the face of looters and modern industrial activity.

Massive road construction programs, strip mining, deep plowing, and inexorable urban development pit archaeologists against governments and business interests throughout the world. "The Rose Affair" tells what happened when the foundations of an Elizabethan theater used by William Shakespeare appeared in the excavations for the basement of a modern high-rise building in the heart of London. The Rose Theater's foundations were eventually sealed beneath a concrete slab, to be excavated and displayed in a museum at some future date, but the controversy surrounding this one

125

site highlights the great complexity of the ethical, financial, and practical issues raised by even minor archaeological finds that lie in the way of modern construction. (At the time of writing, any attempt to excavate the foundations has been stalled by an economic recession.)

Hydroelectric schemes haveposed a threat to archaeological sites since early this century, when a dam across the Nile at Aswan partially flooded the Temple of Isis at Philae, one of the great treasures of ancient Egypt. A loud public outcry was to no avail, but large-scale international efforts through UNESCO did lead to major archaeological surveys in advance of the flooding of Lake Nasser behind the Aswan Dam in the 1960s, when Ramesses II's celebrated Temple at Abu Simbel was moved to higher ground. "Flooding the Maya Heartland" tells a familiar story of a series of priceless archaeological sites threatened by an ambitious hydroelectric scheme undertaken by a government anxious to foster urban development and industrial expansion by generating cheap electric power, without regard to the interests of the local people and a near-pristine rainforest, let alone archaeology. Fighting with minimal resources and even less political clout, archaeologists win surprisingly large numbers of environmental battles, but, even so, the losses to human history are incalculable.

The task of protecting the world's archaeological sites falls, by and large, to governments. No country in the world has the resources to protect even a small proportion of its cultural heritage adequately, especially non-Western states living close to or below the poverty line. But most nations offer at least minimal legal protection to archaeological sites on both private and public lands. The United States is an exception, for individual ownership of land is enshrined in the Constitution. Effectively, this means that the fate of privately owned sites is entirely at the mercy of their owners. Many landowners take their stewardship of the past seriously, but even this is no guarantee that future owners will not consider the profit motive to be more important. As described in "Enlightened Stewardship," the Archaeological Conservancy is a unique organization set up to preserve sites on private land by the simple expedient of purchasing them and preserving them in perpetuity, or working with state or federal authorities to turn them into parks. The Conservancy stands as a success story in a world of archaeology under siege from all manner of uncontrollable, and often destructive, forces.

126

As sites vanish before the bulldozer, more and more archaeologists are spending their careers working with museum collections, and with artifacts excavated and often taken to distant lands many years ago. "Detective Stories" examines this growing kind of archaeology that involves sleuthing worthy of Sherlock Holmes, tracking down collections long in private hands. Who would have suspected, for example, that a major Chumash Indian collection from California would end up in St. Petersburg, Russia, and another in southern Britain? The Chumash collections tell an admirable cautionary tale about the uncertain fate that awaits artifacts when removed from the ground, even with the best intentions in the world.

The past is under siege from collectors and modern industrial activity, and also from tourists. International tourism is the fastest growing business of the late twentieth century, a function of the jumbo jet, the cruise ship, and mass-market packaged travel. "A Wanderer's Lament" was written after a visit to a mobbed Greek temple a mere decade after a more peaceful visit when the weathered ruins had a profound emotional impact on me. One of the great joys of archaeology is the enjoyment of the past on one's own, at sunrise, in the quiet of evening, at moments when deserted sites come alive in your mind, when one's emotions run riot, one's imagination wild. We are in danger of losing the precious emotional impact of ancient times in a sea of package tourism, of feet that erode ancient monuments but seldom pause to allow one to experience their evocative magic.

The eccentric archaeologist is the stuff of cartoons and legends, a benevolent scholar with a bumbling interest in the strange and offbeat. Occasionally, an archaeological research project captures the public imagination and causes a sensation. The recent excavation of moviemaker Cecil B. De Mille's 1920s *The Ten Commandments* movie set on central California's Guadalupe Dunes generated as much international publicity as the discovery of the tomb of the Egyptian pharaoh Tutankhamun in 1922. The reasons are easy to discern. A touch of ancient Egypt, Hollywood excess and the first celluloid epic, and the sheer absurdity of it all touched the public funny bone. Yet the objectives of the research were serious, with the preliminary excavations conducted meticulously using the latest technology. That archaeology does not always deal with the "long ago" and "far away", but is as much about us, our beliefs, and our contemporary world, makes this piece a fitting one to close this volume. ✺

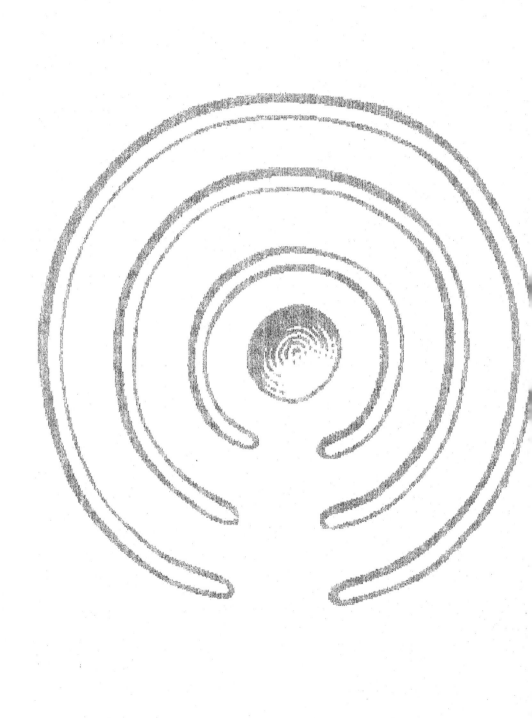

CHAPTER TWENTY-THREE
BLACK DAY
AT SLACK FARM

Like most archaeologists, I have, over the years, developed a numbness to the orgy of site destruction that surrounds us on every side. But a recent story about Slack Farm on the front page of *The Los Angeles Times* has opened old wounds afresh.

"Plunder for Profit," "Looters Rob Old Graves and History"—the headlines leaped out at me with sickening familiarity. But it was only when I read on that I began to realize the full horror of the events at Slack Farm.

The Slack Farm site lies near Uniontown, Kentucky, on land just opposite the confluence of the Ohio and Wabash rivers. The Slack family, which had for many years owned a house and farm at the site, had allowed no digging for artifacts, although on occasion people stole into the corn fields at night to dig illicitly.

Archaeologists had known about the site for years, knew that it was a large, relatively undisturbed Late Mississippian settlement. Judging from surface artifacts, the site dated to sometime between A.D. 1450 and 1650. The farm was of special importance, for it straddled the vital centuries of first European contact with the New World. Cheryl Ann Munson of Indiana University stresses the significance of the farm: she has studied every other large site of this period both up- and downstream. All the other sites have, Munson reports, long since been ravaged by pothunters. Yet through last fall, Slack Farm had, remarkably, remained nearly intact, a unique archive of information about Late Mississippian lifeways.

But no more. With the death of Mrs. Slack the property changed hands. The tenant farmers on the site did make some attempt to keep people from looting the place. In 1987, however, ten pothunters from Kentucky, Indiana, and Illinois paid the new owner of the land $10,000 for the right to "excavate" the site. They rented a tractor and began bulldozing their way through the village midden to reach graves. They pushed heaps of bones aside, and dug through dwellings and the potsherds, hearths, and stone tools associated with them. Along the way, they left detritus of their own—empty pop-top beer and soda cans—scattered on the ground alongside Late Mississippian pottery fragments. Today, Slack Farm looks like a battle-field—a morass of crude shovel holes and gaping trenches. Broken human bones litter the ground, and fractured artifacts crunch under foot.

Two months passed before local residents complained about the dig-ging. Eventually the Kentucky State Police stepped in and arrested the diggers under a state law that prohibits desecrating a venerated object, such as a human grave. The looters pleaded not guilty to the charge—a misde-meanor—and now await trial. But whatever the court decides, the archae-ological damage is done—and it is staggering.

No one knows how many graves were ravaged, what artifacts were removed, what fine pots or funerary ornaments vanished onto the greedy antiquities market. No signs of the dwellings, hearths, and other structures they disturbed remain. A team of archaeologists from the Kentucky Heri-tage Council, Indiana University, and the University of Kentucky, aided by many volunteers, is now trying to assess the damage and record what is left of the site. They are cleaning up the pothunters' holes, recording what intact features remain, and collecting artifact samples to document and date the settlement more precisely.

The ravagers of Slack Farm had no interest in science or prehistory. They were hunting for artifacts for their personal collections and for money. There is a flourishing market in pipes, pendants, whole pots, and other Mississippian grave furnishings. Under these circumstances, pothunting can be addictive.

Prehistoric artifact prices are staggering, and rising steeply as the illegal supply—especially from overseas—becomes scarcer. A stone ax can fetch as much as $1,000, a pipe up to $5,000. A looter who finds a rare type of Mississippian pottery bottle or an embossed copper plate can name his price, and expect to get it. The marketplace is so hungry for antiquities of every kind that a lively underground market in very high quality forgeries grows daily.

Slack Farm, Kentucky. Aerial photograph of the damage wrought by looters. Photograph: Kenny Barkley, Union County, Kentucky. Courtesy: Kentucky Heritage Council. Reprinted with permission.

In some ways, one can hardly blame landowners for cashing in on the potential of such hidden treasures. They lease rights to companies to mine their land for coal. Why not lease rights to pothunters to dig for artifacts? Both coal and artifacts can be regarded as wealth underfoot. But in the case of the prehistoric past the issues are much more complex.

This point was underlined for me when I showed the newspaper account of the Slack Farm tragedy to some friends at a coffee break. I was horrified by some of the reactions. "So what?" shrugged one coffee shop acquaintance. "It's a free country." He expressed what turned out to be a widely held view: it's up to landowners what they do with their property. In my numbness, I had forgotten that many people see nothing wrong with private landowners ravaging the past for profit—as long as laws are not broken.

We have a strange relationship with the prehistoric past in this country. Most Americans, like my friends, have no direct cultural identification or emotional tie with North American prehistory, with Mesa Verde, Cahokia,

131

or the many other brilliant achievements of the American Indian. As far as most people are concerned, history (and North American archaeology, for that matter) began with Leif Erikson, Christopher Columbus, and the Pilgrim Fathers. Anything that predates European contact is considered somewhat irrelevant, and often ignored in school.

So most Americans of non-Indian descent tend to think of prehistoric Indian sites in impersonal, remote ways. Most would protest vigorously at the destruction of an important, privately owned, historic site from pioneer days, or shudder at the very thought of someone looting their neighbor's great-grandmother's grave. But a long-abandoned prehistoric Indian village and the graves of the people who once lived there are a different matter.

It would be naive to think that Slack Farm is an isolated incident. Looting and pothunting have been endemic in the Southeast since the Depression days of the 1930s, and were rife in the Southwest in the early years of this century. Reports from elsewhere in Kentucky, and from Illinois, Indiana, and Ohio, testify to widespread vandalism directed against archaeological sites of every time period over the entire length of the Ohio Valley.

But there is far more to the Slack Farm tragedy than the material destruction of hundreds of prehistoric graves—or of an entire archaeological site. For days after reading the news stories, I was haunted by the staggering scientific loss at Slack Farm.

To understand the dimensions of that loss one must realize that the Mississippian culture was a brilliant efflorescence of late prehistoric life in the Midwest and the South. Cahokia, Moundville, and other great centers testify to that culture's extraordinary elaboration of public constructions and brilliant art traditions in ceramics, copper, and shell. The first Mississippian communities appeared after A.D. 750, at just about the time when maize farming took hold in eastern North America. Mississippian culture was past its apogee in many regions when Europeans first penetrated the Midwest in the seventeenth century.

Many questions about this ancient society remain unanswered. Most excavations have focused, fairly naturally, on a few town sites and their mounds and spectacular monuments. Very few villages or cemeteries have been investigated—especially with the full apparatus of modern, hi-tech archaeology. The well-preserved deposits at Slack Farm offered one of the few chances for such a painstaking investigation.

As in other Mississippian communities, the people who lived at Slack Farm probably enjoyed close and constant economic, political, and social relationships with other villages and hamlets up and down the Ohio. But most of these sites also have been destroyed by looters. Until this tragedy, Slack Farm had been our best chance to study the dynamics of this Mississippian society.

Some of the fine Mississippian pots from Slack Farm so coveted by collectors are identical to vessels made in Arkansas, far from the Ohio Valley. Some of the copper and marine shell ornaments prized by looters attest to even more distant trade—for copper either with the Great Lakes area or the Appalachians, for marine shells with the Atlantic or Gulf coasts.

It may be news to looters, but the fragmentary bones they cast aside are a treasure trove of potential information on Mississippian diet and disease, of vital genetic data about the biological relationships between prehistoric Americans, of evidence on ancient warfare. We now have the scientific techniques to probe such questions. Unfortunately, most of the vital clues for doing so vanished when the site was destroyed.

Slack Farm straddles the vital centuries of European contact with American Indians. We know this because glass beads, brass tinklers, and other European artifacts have come from the surface of the ravaged settlement. These finds testify to some form of indirect, or perhaps even direct, contact between the Slack Farm people and early European traders and explorers. Studying such imports requires a detailed knowledge of their precise archaeological context. The looted holes at Slack Farm remind us that we may never understand the true nature of these early contacts.

Christopher Columbus's quincentennial has passed, yet we still know little about the complex relationships between Europeans and Native Americans five centuries ago. What changes in culture resulted from European contact? Did exotic diseases decimate midwestern populations? Were the Late Mississippians in the Ohio Valley the ancestors of one of the historic tribes of the Midwest and Southeast? What goods were traded between whites and Indians, and how did this new trade affect relationships between indigenous societies? The looted burials and village deposits at Slack Farm might have helped find some of the answers to these questions. They cannot help us now.

When historians look back at the history of archaeology in the late twentieth century, they will be struck by a tragic irony. The seventies and eighties were the decades when archaeologists finally developed the scientific technology to attack fundamental questions about the past. Yet the same scientists were powerless to stem the tidal wave of destruction that swept away the very data they could now study to its full potential.

The only bright side of the Slack Farm affair is the public outcry aroused locally by the looting. This protest led to new state legislation in Kentucky, which now makes it a felony to desecrate a human grave, regardless of the race or antiquity of the person buried. Yet, in Indiana similar legislative efforts failed. In surrounding states, no one is tackling the legal, ethical, and archaeological problem of site vandalism.

It's not making front page headlines, but looting on the scale of Slack Farm is commonplace in nearly every state—from the Bering Strait to the U.S. Virgin Islands, especially on private lands. The fact is that we and our friends are not making enough noise about this insidious scandal society tolerates in its midst. No one else is going to do it for us, so we had better raise our voices very loudly before it is too late.

In a way I feel like Nero, blithely fiddling while Rome burns. Only this time it is not Rome that is at stake, but the priceless and finite past. The Slack Farm affair has made me wonder for the first time if, perhaps, it is already too late.

AN UPDATE ON THE SLACK FARM SITE

Archaeological investigation of the damaged areas of the village and its cemeteries followed the arrest of the looters and demonstrated that they disturbed more than 700 burials. Despite the extensive damage to the site, the archaeological work showed that the looters were stopped before much of the residential areas and the smaller cemeteries were destroyed. Additionally, archaeologists recovered new information concerning the lifestyles of the late Mississippian people who occupied this site and neighboring settlements along the Ohio River. Analysis of the materials and records from the site is ongoing, and there is a great deal of local interest in preserving the Slack Farm site as a unique protohistoric Mississippian village.

Though initial legislative efforts to prevent looting were met in the Indiana legislature by successful protests from artifact collectors, continued looting changed the laws there too. Less than a year after the Slack Farm depredations, illicit diggers struck again nearby. This time their target was a Hopewell Mound (the GE Mound) on the Indiana site of the Ohio River. Once newspapers picked up the story, the public outcry that followed the Slack Farm looting was renewed. As a consequence, Indiana's governor signed a law in the spring of 1989 that was designed to help land managers and landowners protect burial sites and other types of archaeological sites on public or private lands from illicit excavation and from accidental damage. Changes in laws have not brought an end to looting in Indiana and Kentucky, of course, but we believe the incidence of destruction has begun to decline thanks to continued public concern. ❉

David Pollack
Kentucky Heritage Council, Frankfort

Cheryl Ann Munson
Department of Anthropology, Indiana University, Bloomington

CHAPTER TWENTY-FOUR

THE ROSE AFFAIR

Humble foundations, part of an audience pit, portions of a small stage—hardly the kind of archaeological finds that would unleash a torrent of passionate protest. Yet they did, when construction of a new building threatened the remnants of Shakespeare's Rose Theater on London's South Bank. "It is like demolishing the Parthenon to make way for a car park. . ." cried the more than 3,000 actors and other protesters who gathered at the building site where the Elizabethan theater's foundations lay exposed. Columnist Peter Simple of the *Daily Telegraph* proclaimed that "if our culture today were truly alive, and creating plays even as good as *Titus Andronicus*, no one would think twice about preserving such a dismal patch of mud." The Rose affair soon became classic archaeological theater. Conservationists, actors, and archaeologists were pitted against developers and those who dismissed the muddied remains under the rising office block as not worth all the fuss.

London is in the throes of a construction boom, fueled both by soaring property prices as well as its own emergence as a major financial center for the European Community. Inevitably, this has led to the rapid demise of the city's earlier incarnations, of which there have been many. Recently, this destruction of valuable archaeological data has spread to theatrically Sacred Ground—on the south bank of the Thames near Southwark Bridge, where four Elizabethan theaters once stood: the Rose, built in about 1587 and demolished in 1606, the Swan (1595), the Globe (most famous of all), constructed in 1599, and the Hope (1613). Christopher Marlowe's plays were first performed at the Rose. Shakespeare's *Titus Andronicus* and *Henry VI* came to the stage there. It is believed that Shakespeare himself may have been a young actor in Lord Strange's Company, which performed at the Rose in 1592. Theatrically sacred ground indeed . . .

What did the Rose look like? Unfortunately, we have little contemporary evidence to go on. A few London panoramas and a sketch of the interior of the Swan in 1596 provide limited and conflicting perspectives. Therein lies the importance of the newly discovered foundations, for these unspectacular remains provide the first reliable evidence for the actual layout of an Elizabethan theater. Combined with the surviving diaries of the Rose's owner Philip Henslowe, they are a unique archive of theatrical history.

Although the location of the Rose was known in general terms, it wasn't until a 1957 office building was torn down early last year to make room for a new structure that its precise location was confirmed. Portions of the theater had already been destroyed when pilings were sunk for the 1957 building. Laboring for five painstaking months under the pressure of construction deadlines, Museum of London archaeologists uncovered a small, polygonal structure, with either 16 or 18 sides. The audience at the Rose had stood in a central pit, which was open to the elements. The pit was only 43 feet wide and paved with mortar. It cost one a penny to stand there, two pence to enjoy the play from the gallery. Here the more affluent sat under cover, protected from the rain by a thatched roof that slightly overhung the pit.

In about 1592, the theater was remodeled to permit a larger audience in the pit. The stage was moved back 16 feet, and the theater was expanded to the north, turning from a polygon into a closed horseshoe. More people could enjoy the plays, but the covered stage was never larger, only 16 to 20 feet from back to front, perhaps 36 to 40 feet wide.

The discovery of the Rose caused a public sensation and an extraordinary outpouring of thespian emotion. Immediate demands were made for preservation. To their credit, Imry Merchant Developers, PLC, the owners of the property, promptly announced they would leave the 1957 piles in position, so as not to endanger the theater further by their removal. They also agreed to relocate their new pilings outside the perimeter of the theater as well as to backfill the site over a fiberglass net intended to preserve the already exposed foundations. But the developers' plan was not enough for those filled with the spirit of the Bard. The day backfilling was to begin, protesters surrounded the site and blocked access, demanding that the site be listed as a scheduled monument, with the same protection granted such sites as Stonehenge and Maiden Castle. Without scheduled monument status, the future of the Rose was uncertain. Shakespearean actor Ian McKellen led an on-site vigil, and Dustin Hoffman made an appeal for preservation in an on-stage appearance in London's West End. Construction stopped. After urgent Parliamentary debate, the Government intervened and agreed to pay the developers one million pounds compensation for a 30-day delay while options were discussed.

The debate over options proceeded against a background of swirling controversy. Should the recent discoveries be displayed to the public with only limited further excavation? Or should the site be completely excavated, with the objective of meticulously documenting the architectural features of the Rose and then allowing the parcel of land to be developed? Archaeological observers like Martin Biddle, famous for his excavations of medieval Winchester, argued for immediate excavation. Other archaeologists advocated limited excavation, then display. Meanwhile, the actors held out passionately for complete excavation *and* preservation of the site, "of the very boards where the immortal Bard once trod."

The negotiations over the fate of the Rose were conducted within the framework of British Law and a Code of Practice drawn up between the British Property Federation and archaeologists some years ago. Under this legislation, developers are entitled to compensation should the government retract or alter construction permits that have already been granted. In the case of the Rose, English Heritage pushed for a building plan that would not only preserve the theater's remains but would allow for the site's future public display. To English Heritage's and Imry Merchant's credit, an agreement was reached. Imry Merchant not only agreed to redesign the building around the theater but included a public viewing area in their plans as well. According to current plans, the new structure will sit on a "bridge" across the pilings, leaving the remains of the Rose intact in a 20-foot-high workspace under the building. The excavation of the site is expected to resume after the new office building is completed. Meanwhile, precautions have been taken to keep the soil around the theater biologically and chemically stable; the exposed remains have been photodocumented and encased in a multilayered shell to prevent further decay.

The Rose affair has raised a fundamental question—when does one preserve, when does one record, then destroy, or, as in the case of the Rose, excavate and then make provisions for future public display? It is a debate that archaeologists everywhere frequently confront. Hydroelectric schemes in Syria, urban renewal in Cape Town, deep plowing in Arkansas, office buildings in London—the problem is basically the same anywhere, and there are no easy answers.

Without question, the Rose was saved because a considerable number of important and influential people both on stage and off felt an emotional bond with the site. The actors who were most vocal claimed that they felt the spirit of Shakespeare reaching out to them from the ground. We would be rash to mock such feelings. They come to all of us who love the past at some time—on a moonlit night in the amphitheater at Epidauros when Euripidean stanzas float on the breeze, with the first snow at Mesa Verde, when viewing a Stone Age engraving deep in a Dordogne cave by flickering candlelight.

Emotion apart, there are also major economic reasons for preserving the site. Britain's heritage is a major tourist attraction and a major money maker. As the brilliant reconstruction of Viking York has shown, there is good money to be made from archaeology well displayed. However, the Rose will face healthy competition from the Tower of London, Westminister Abbey, and the British Museum, to say nothing of actor Sam Wanamaker's Globe Theatre replica due to open just a short distance from the Rose's office-building home. It is not uncharitable to describe Wanamaker's Globe project as history with a touch of Disneyland about it, in the shadow of which the remains of the Rose will certainly pale. In any case, the Rose has been saved.

The issue, however, remains—to what extent should vast sums of money be spent to develop archaeological sites for public viewing because "they evoke the spirit of the past," especially in a country where funds for archaeological research are limited. The Rose may be a theatrical Parthenon, but it would have been better and cheaper to excavate the site in meticulous, fine-grained detail, and to settle for permanent historical information rather than the display of the rather unspectacular remains as a tribute to the Bard. ❀

CHAPTER TWENTY-FIVE
FLOODING THE
MAYA HEARTLAND

Years ago I was on a flight from Aswan to the temple of Abu Simbel in Upper Eygpt. Our plane skirted the western shore of Lake Nasser, swooping low past the colossal statues of Ramesses on the temple's imposing facade. I had come to Abu Simbel in the footsteps of the energetic and highly successful Giovanni Belzoni, who dug away the sand mantling the temple in 1819. It was a frustrating visit because the shimmering waters of Lake Nasser were no substitute for the temple's original setting, which overlooked a narrow, densely cultivated valley hemmed in by a harsh desert. As I gazed up at Ramesses and then stared out over the lake, I contemplated the astounding damage done, not by the tomb-robber of yesteryear, but by hydroelectric schemes of all kinds. The Aswan Dam project flooded thousands of square miles of archaeologically virgin territory. Fortunately, a UNESCO rescue campaign moved Abu Simbel to higher ground. And at least an effort was made to recover some of the rich archaeological remains that had lain along the now-flooded river banks.

Hydroelectric schemes have dealt harsh blows to archaeology in all corners of the world. The Upper Volta Dam in Ghana, large-scale engineering works on the Euphrates River in Syria, the Army Corps of Engineers' many dams in North America, and, the grandfather of them all, the Kariba Dam that straddles the Middle Zambezi Valley in central Africa— all have inundated priceless archives of the past. And in most cases archaeologists had to scramble to save what they could.

Now we hear of another ambitious hydroelectric scheme, this time on the Usumacinta River that separates Mexico and Guatemala. The river flows through a heavily forested region in the heartland of ancient Maya civilization. On its banks lie the great Maya centers at Piedras Negras and

Yaxchilán. Guatemala and Mexico began studies for a huge joint dam project in 1980, but public protests, a guerilla movement, and technical problems delayed the project again and again. The final plan calls for two to four dams that would produce between 2 and 3.7 megawatts of electricity, greatly exceeding Guatemala's current and future needs. The project would inundate as much as 507 square miles, mostly in Guatemala. Project engineers favor a high water level as this reduces the cost of producing electrical power.

In May 1989, Mexico's Salinas administration announced the project had been canceled because of Guatemalan concerns about the destruction of precious archaeological sites on their side of the river. The Guatemalan side of the river is still covered by the Lacandón rain forest, so the ecological impact of a Mexican dam would be felt dramatically by its neighbor. In contrast, as the local population rose sharply in Mexico, especially in nearby Chiapas, nearly 70 percent of the forest had been destroyed by 1990. Mexicans living in burgeoning rural communities have a need for electricity, and irrigation farming could feed many families, so local pressure for the dam scheme is mounting. In February 1992, President Salinas traveled to Guatemala for discussions about supplying electric power using a Usumacinta dam based entirely on Mexican soil. The Mexican authorities have assured the Guatemalans that the project will not affect them, but many outsiders are skeptical. Since then, a cloak of secrecy has descended over the project. President Salinas is said to have "suspended" the project. Other Mexican sources claim that a long-term financing deal has been arranged with the Inter-American Bank (not the World Bank, which has declined to participate), and that the project will go ahead. In short, the fate of the dam is anyone's guess, but archaeologists cannot afford to relax.

The destructive potential of the dam in ecological terms is enormous, for the still relatively pristine Usumacinta River is crucial to the ecology of the Lacandón rain forest. And many intact sites lie near the river, which is already heavily traveled by "eco-adventure" tourist groups. Even with partial inundation, the archaeological losses would be incalculable. Piedras Negras and Yaxchilán are well known, but not thoroughly excavated. Also, the heavy forest cover and political unrest have hindered archaeological exploration of the surrounding country.

Piedras Negras is famous for its sculpture and architecture, for art works that were influenced by many styles, like those of Palenque and the northeastern Petén. The great Mayanist Tatiana Proskouriakoff studied the intricately carved stelae at the site and discovered that they recorded the names of individual rulers and their dates of birth, accession to power, conquests, and so on. The central precinct of Piedras Negras lies on a natural hill, but even the lowest flood levels would turn the site into a series of islands and peninsulas. The South Group buildings, which may be the center of the little known Early Classic occupation at Piedras Negras, would be lost. The water would also inundate the unsurveyed low areas around the site.

Yaxchilán lies on the western bank, with clusters of buildings arranged on natural, terraced hills and some on lower ground near the river. Once gleaming with red paint, the buildings, famous for their Late Classic sculpture and carved lintels, ascend in rows against forest-shrouded hills. With its unique setting and luxuriant vegetation, Yaxchilán is the most evocative Maya site I have ever visited. We know that Lord Progenitor-Jaguar founded a long-lived dynasty here on August 2, A.D. 320. His descendants rule until Yaxchilán was abandoned 500 years later. Three possible dam locations lie on the large river bend where Yaxchilán once flourished, one at the site itself. Some dam configurations would result in the flooding of all structures on the river bank. The area around Yaxchilán, which undoubtedly includes dozens of towns and villages, is virtually unexplored and would vanish under water.

As Mayanist after Mayanist has pointed out, to explore Maya cities out of context of their surrounding communities is meaningless. But research on these less spectacular sites is vitally important. Such work at Copán and Tikal and many other sites is helping revolutionize our knowledge of Maya society. If dams are built, Piedras Negras and Yaxchilán will be little more than architectural footnotes to Maya civilization.

Quite apart from the destruction at these major sites, the damage to smaller Maya settlements will be catastrophic. Such well-known sites as Altar de Sacrificios and Planchon de las Figuras, where a huge riverside limestone slab bears formal inscriptions and dozens of graffiti-like carvings, are threatened. It would be naive to assume that archaeologists can stop the Usumacinta project—and we can bet that dams will be built, if not immediately, at some point in the future. Only recently have archaeologists had any representation on the commissions overseeing planning, and even that representation is minimal.

There seems to be little that anyone can do except to apply political pressure at the highest levels. The American Anthropological Association and the Society for American Archaeology have protested the dam scheme. The German Ethnological Society has expressed strong concern at the diplomatic level.

Dam projects are always controversial. Their supporters claim they will bring long-term benefits to both industrial and private users in distant cities as well as to the surrounding local population, who will have electric light and water for irrigation for the first time. They forget the enormous emotional and economic hardships imposed in the areas to be flooded. But there is a case to be made that large-scale hydroelectric power is a powerful catalyst for rural and industrial development, and for reducing chronic poverty in less developed countries.

On the Usumacinta, however, the cultural price may be too high. Are we to lose forever much of Piedras Negras and its remains of once flourishing kingdoms? Who will visit the terraced city of Yaxchilán if much of it is under water? Such questions carry little weight with politicians and engineers concerned with economic feasibility studies and industrial development studies that will determine the future of the Usumacinta project.

There is still time to take action, to express outrage and concern, and to lobby for proper financial support of archaeological work. We should insist that enough of the mammoth construction budget (reportedly between $2.1 and 3.7 billion) be allocated to allow proper excavation, recording, and archaeological survey with adequate lead time. ☀

CHAPTER TWENTY-SIX
ENLIGHTENED STEWARDSHIP

Federal and state laws give a measure of protection to archaeological and historic sites on public lands, and have resulted in the successful prosecution of several high-profile looting cases. But privately owned sites survive at the whim of their owners, with virtually no protection. The effect of tougher laws and more vigorous enforcement has been to divert looters and professional pothunters onto private lands. In many parts of the country archaeology is losing ground. Prices for fine Native American artifacts on the international antiquities market are rising. Inevitably, there are landowners only too eager to sell artifacts from their properties to the highest bidder with a backhoe.

"Saving the Past for the Future" has become a popular slogan in archaeological circles. But how does one do this on private lands? Fortunately, public awareness of the importance of archaeology is much improved over a generation ago. The Indiana Jones movies, more exposure in the media, and efforts at public education by the profession have all played their part. Big-budget movies such as *Black Robe* and *Dances with Wolves* have placed Native Americans at center stage. The 1990 Native American Graves Protection and Repatriation Act has also drawn attention to the complex relationship between archaeologists and Native Americans (see *Archaeology*, November/December 1994). We live in an era of rising respect for Native American culture, values, and achievements. Many property owners feel a deep respect and responsibility for archaeological sites on their land. Some states, notably Kentucky, have developed successful pledge schemes in which landowners promise to protect sites on their property. But such promises only last the lifetime of the owner—there are no long-term guarantees. Only one strategy is effective: continuous ownership and stewardship. This is the mandate of a remarkable organization, the Archaeological Conservancy.

Founded in 1980 by a group of private citizens and archaeologists dedicated to protecting the future of the past, the Archaeological Conservancy's mission resembles that of the much higher profile Nature Conservancy, but with a fraction of its resources. In purchasing privately owned sites, the Conservancy agrees to maintain them for the public on a permanent basis. President Mark Michel and his small staff operate out of a headquarters in Albuquerque and regional offices in Duluth, Georgia; Groveport, Ohio; and Sacramento, California, with a minuscule budget of $850,000 a year. In 14 years they have acquired 100 sites in 22 states. Their acquisitions range from Paleo-Indian sites to an early nineteenth-century Hudson's Bay Company trading fort.

The Conservancy's first purchase was Powers Fort, Missouri, a Mississippian cultural-civic-ceremonial center consisting of a small village and four mounds surrounded by an earthen embankment, dating to ca. A.D. 1350. Soon afterward, it acquired Savage Cave, Kentucky, where 18 feet of deposits extend into Paleo-Indian times. The Conservancy owns, or has owned, sites at Borax Lake, California; the Hopewell Mounds Group and Stackhouse Mound—a large, nearly pristine Adena mound complex—in Ohio; and Pueblo San Marcos, New Mexico, whose inhabitants once controlled the nearby Cerrillos turquoise mines. It is also responsible for five preserves in heavily looted areas of Texas and Oklahoma, where the mound-building Caddo culture flourished between ca A.D. 700 and the mid-eighteenth century. Each spans a different Caddo period, allowing a continued research on this most important of early American chiefdoms. The 100th property, obtained in late 1994, is the three-acre Lamb Spring site near Littleton, Colorado, a Paleo-Indian hunting and game-processing area that may be one of the earliest of its kind in the United States.

The Conservancy accepts sites as gifts, and works closely with land developers whose projects impinge on prehistoric and historic sites. They have achieved some remarkable successes. In 1993 the Weyerhauser Real Estate Company was developing a planned community on the site of Fort Nisqually, a Hudson's Bay Company trading post founded in 1832. The Conservancy persuaded Weyerhauser to set aside the open space in the heart of its new community. E. I. duPont de Nemours Company donated an archaeological easement on the site of Old Mobile, Alabama, the first French settlement at Mobile (1702–1711). Such transactions benefit not only archaeology, but the developer, who receives a tax break and, more important, a positive public image. In other cases, the Conservancy purchases sites outright for the appraised value of the land. The funds come from its 13,000 members, corporate sponsors, and private foundations. In purchasing the Lamb Spring site, the Conservancy collaborated with the Denver Museum of Natural History. The two organizations raised matching funds against a grant of $100,000 from the Colorado State Historical Fund.

The Conservancy staff works closely with a national board of archaeologists, with interested lay people, and with local committees that recommend sites for acquisition. Native Americans serve on both the national and regional advisory boards, and the Conservancy consults closely with tribes before acquiring any site. Mark Michel spends much of his time traveling around the country, looking at prospective acquisitions and working with property owners, sometimes over several years, before purchasing a site. With 100 acquisitions to its credit, the Conservancy is a viable option for preservation-minded landowners who wish to sell their land. The Conservancy assumes it will own sites in perpetuity, but sometimes transfers them to a national or state agency to be developed into protected public parks. Such was the case with the Hopewell Mounds Group in Ohio, now part of the Hopewell Culture National Historical Park. The Conservancy approves research projects that have specific goals and are compatible with conservation of the site. For example, study of animal bone fractures at the Lamb Spring site may yield evidence of very early human occupation, perhaps before 9500 B.C.

The Archaeological Conservancy strategy *works*, and the in final analysis it is the best option archaeologists have in this country to insure permanent protection of sites on private land. The Conservancy is at a point of critical mass, where future growth and public support are likely to be exponential. Mark Michel hopes that large bequests will put the Conservancy's endowment and activities on a new footing. What better investment in the future of the United States than to help save its past. I urge everyone, archaeologist and nonarchaeologist, to join and support the Conservancy in its unique and highly successful work. 🏵️

CHAPTER TWENTY-SEVEN

DETECTIVE STORIES

During the course of the Gulf War, Saddam Hussein's generals parked their fighter planes, tanks, and artillery on Mesopotamian tells, and in response we pounded these targets with countless bombs. One direct hit could have destroyed more artifacts than generations of clandestine diggers might have collected. All this is quite apart from Saddam Hussein's depredations to the Kuwait Museum—its many treasures were spirited off to Baghdad. The cynic in me wonders how long it will be before many of Kuwait's choice artifacts appear on the international market, dispersed to the far corners of the globe. This will not be the first time that precious artifacts have met with such a fate.

Many years ago, I wanted to examine a collection of Stone Age artifacts dating to about 7800 B.C. from Peacock's Farm in eastern England. This remarkable collection of 35 tiny arrow barbs and stone blades, found deep in East Anglian peat, was one of the first Stone Age assemblages to be radiocarbon dated. In those days, known Stone Age sites were few and far between in Britain, and dated collections were even rarer. To my astonishment, the curator's assistant told me that only half of the collection was still in Cambridge—the remainder of it had been exchanged with a museum in Sydney, Australia.

Until that moment I had assumed that collections stayed together in one institution. How wrong I was. Today, tracing missing collections requires a new generation of archaeological detectives capable of excavating not in the soil but in the basements of obscure and not-so-obscure museums.

The late Travis Hudson, for some very productive years the archaeologist at the Santa Barbara Museum of Natural History, was a master of such sleuthing. The Santa Barbara Museum has an internationally famous collection of baskets and other artifacts made by the Chumash Indians of southern California. Only a handful of Chumash were left when the eccentric but gifted Smithsonian anthropologist John Harrington set out to record their language and customs in the early 1920s. His extraordinary diaries and field notes provide a wealth of information on the culture of the expert fisherfolk and sea-mammal hunters who had exploited the rich fisheries of the Santa Barbara Channel region for more than 3,000 years— they were eventually decimated by exotic European diseases and draconian resettlement policies. Harrington's notes are so complete that Hudson and his colleagues were able to reconstruct a Chumash canoe from his descriptions.

Inspired by Harrington, Hudson and his close colleague Thomas Blackburn collaborated in tracking down collections of California Indian artifacts and basketry in museums far from Santa Barbara. They faced an appallingly difficult task. With minimal funds and unending patience, Blackburn and Hudson assumed the role of archaeological Sherlock Holmeses. They wrote letters, made phone calls, and visited museums near and far. There were no computerized data banks on California Indian artifacts or microfilmed records of museum card catalogs, just dozens of tantalizing leads buried in explorers' diaries, government records, and Harrington's notes. Hudson started by developing a history of collectors in the Santa Barbara region, then followed their collections as far afield as Australia and the Soviet Union.

While the California Academy of Sciences had collected substantial amounts of ethnographic material early on, most of it was lost in the earthquake of 1906, leaving the best collections overseas. Some of the finest collections of California basketry, including forms and designs unknown in American collections, are in the Soviet Union. The Russian-American Company once had been very active in the fur trade on the coast, and Russian naval officers collected many artifacts from native peoples. "Their headdress, made of feathers, can be said to display great taste," wrote V. M. Golovnin, who collected material around San Francisco Bay in 1818. Beginning in 1849, the Gold Rush brought a flood of polyglot visitors to California, some of them collectors and excavators. Chumash middens were trenched, and their precious artifacts were shipped out to private collectors and museums alike. Within museum circles and among the cognoscenti there was a positive frenzy for Indian hats and baskets.

Even then, the journeys of California Indian artifacts were not over. Consider the collection of the wealthy financier William Blackmore, who acquired many priceless artifacts from the western United States in the late nineteenth century. He donated his collections to the Salisbury Museum in southern England. After his death in 1929, the museum decided to deacquisition the Blackmore holdings since its focus was really on the history of Salisbury. Henry Beasley, a private collector, acquired the ethnographic specimens, while the British Museum purchased the archaeological material. After Beasley's death, his collections, too, were parceled out—to museums in Cambridge, Liverpool, and London.

Other California collections wound up in overseas museums as a result of routine exchanges between museums, or loans. At some museums, the process of exchange often reflected the specific interests of a particular curator. Eric Douglas, a curator at the Denver Art Museum, had a strong interest in Oceanic art and regularly exchanged Native American artifacts for better Oceanic specimens. As a result, notable collections of California Indian basketry now reside in London, Oxford, Edinburgh, Ghent, Göteborg, Stockholm, and Helsinki.

Travis Hudson, a talented scholar, was tenacious in his quest to ferret out lost collections of Indian artifacts. "I'm working with an international archive of traditional culture," he once told me before his untimely death in 1988. His colleague Thomas Blackburn helped in the research and has recently pulled together the results in monograph form. It is one of those publications that only a handful of people will ever read, but it is a fascinating one.

Therein lies the rub. Archaeologists are seen as excavators and fieldworkers, as people of action and adventure. Indeed, many of the professional rewards for archaeologists lie in the spectacular excavation and notable discoveries that hit the pages of the newspapers and magazines. But what happens to the archaeological record once it ends up in a museum collection? And what about the myriad private collections that lie in attics, basements, and cabinets throughout the world? As undisturbed sites vanish, much of tomorrow's research will shift from the field into dusty storerooms, auction houses, and private homes, as archaeologists become historical Hercule Poirots in search of lost artifacts and vanished collections.

Blackburn not only collaborated in the research, but wrote most of the resulting monograph, *Time's Flotsam*. I read it the day the Gulf War started and was tempted to wonder if, one day, a twenty-first-century sequel will describe the fate of Kuwait's collections. ☼

CHAPTER TWENTY-EIGHT
A WANDERER'S LAMENT

We anchored off Agia Marina at the northeastern corner of the island of Aegina on a calm September afternoon. High above us, on the crest of a hill, the Temple of Aphaia stood beckoning in the brilliant sunshine. We followed a narrow, winding path through hillside olive groves and savored the smell of pine needles that I will always associate with classical sites in Greece. There was no sound except the occasional birdcall or the gentle rustling of the sea breeze in the trees. The temple was deserted that lazy September day 11 years ago, its caretakers yawning in their small kiosk. We lingered for several hours, wandering through the temple, watching the lengthening shadows of its columns on the worn stone floor. Around us, the panorama of Salamis, the Peloponnese, Attica, and the blue ocean became softer, the folds of distant hills lying in ever deeper evening shadows. The air was warm and still, and the setting sun cast a magnificent rosy light on the ancient temple.

A few days later, we anchored in the shelter of the Temple of Poseidon at Sounion, as countless small ships had done before us. An hour before sunset, we stood beside its brilliant white, salt-encrusted columns. We had the place to ourselves except for an English couple in sensible tweeds and walking shoes. They sat to one side and read from a guidebook while we searched for Lord Byron's name on the columns. The setting sun bathed Sounion in pink, mystical hues. We asked the English couple back to the boat to drink wine, and read aloud from the *Odyssey* until the moon rose over the hills.

We visited the amphitheater at Epidauros, which cast its magic spell. I sat on the highest tier of seats in the hot sun and listened to a German professor recite Euripides to his students. They were well schooled in the poet, joining in with the chorus to the professor's evident delight. I listened with closed eyes.

A few months ago an opportunity arose to revisit those magical sites. I jumped at the chance, tantalizing my companions with accounts of the magic of Aphaia, Sounion, and Epidauros. When we reached Aegina, I could hardly wait to rent a motor scooter and return to Aphaia's shrine. But this time the magic was gone. For one thing, the parking lot was jammed with tour buses. We choked on diesel fumes. The temple itself was cordoned off; one could not wander among the columns. At one point we had the temple more or less to ourselves when a crescendo of laboring motors brought another busload of tourists, and the chance for solitude was gone.

I left depressed. The visit had hardly been an elevating experience. Even when the tour buses were gone and the site was quiet, the sense of communion with the past eluded me. Back aboard ship, I took out my well-thumbed copy of Rose Macaulay's *The Pleasure of Ruins*, which I consider, together with Homer, to be an essential traveler's companion in Greece. It was comforting to find her lamenting the "excavated, tidied up monuments of the world." Like her, I envied one Colonel P. M. Skyes, who in 1914 rode his horse up the great staircase at Persepolis, so overwhelmed had he been by the view. An Englishman named Robert Byron (no relation to the poet) subsequently rode up the stairs and camped there, "while the columns and winged beasts kept their solitude beneath the stars, and not a sound or movement disturbed the empty moonlit plain." Byron returned some years later by car and was bitterly disappointed by the clouds of dust from passing trucks, and by the excavations that had cleaned up the site.

Epidauros was equally disappointing. No Euripides this time. The theater was crowded with a polyglot crowd of tourists, including a group of French high school girls sunbathing topless. I fled to a deserted ruin field and found a measure of peace.

Perhaps my generation was one of the last to be able to enjoy the world's great archaeological sites in solitude—Stonehenge in the evening, the serried ramparts of Maiden Castle at full moon, the Great Enclosure at Zimbabwe at dawn. I suspect that today's generation has little opportunity to absorb the full impact of these ruins. Ten years ago, just the smell of pine trees at Aphaia was enough to recall what it must have been like back in 1810 when antiquarian Charles Cockerell and his young friends camped among the ruins, dug up and removed the fallen carvings from its pediments, and dined off wild partridges, roast lamb, strong retsina, and raki.

The local villagers "lightened our toil with the rustic lyre, the song and the dance." Today, the site is sanitized, sterile, and overwhelmed by multitudes of visitors.

Do not misunderstand me. I am all for international tourism that promotes an understanding of archaeology and a heightened appreciation of our common cultural heritage, especially when it contributes to developing national economies. But, increasingly, both casual tourists and more serious visitors are enjoying places like Epidauros and Sounion less and less, simply because these sites have absorbed about as many people as they can. So I can hardly blame one member of our party for remarking that she did not want to go to Delphi because it would be "just another pile of rocks." The archaeologist in me shuddered, but the tourist in me sympathized.

I confess that I too would like to ride a horse up the staircase at Persepolis and to explore the American Southwest on a mule. But I'll probably have to settle for a quick visit to Aphaia when it first opens in the morning, before the crowds gather and before the site is engulfed by diesel fumes. Even then, I fear the once savored aura of this special place will continue to elude me. ☀

CHAPTER TWENTY-NINE
DIGGING DE MILLE

In his autobiography, filmmaker Cecil B. De Mille writes: "If, 1,000 years from now, archaeologists happen to dig beneath the sands of Guadalupe [in central California], I hope that they do not rush into print with the amazing news that Egyptian civilization, far from being confined to the Valley of the Nile, extended all the way to the Pacific Coast of North America. The sphinxes they will find were buried there when we had finished with them and dismantled our huge set of the gates of Pharaoh's city."

Filmed in 1923, De Mille's *The Ten Commandments* was one of the first major Hollywood epics and cost the then enormous sum of 1.4 million dollars. DeMille retold the story of Moses and the Exodus on a truly monumental scale, complete with the parting of the Red Sea. Combing the Pacific Coast for a suitable desert location for his Pharaonic city, De Mille chose one of the remote Guadalupe dunes overlooking the Pacific. Set designer Paul Iribe, later the father of Art Deco in Paris, created there an ancient Egyptian city that was a curious mixture of Abu Simbel, Karnak, and other Nile temples. De Mille assembled a mammoth army of 1,000 construction workers to build the gargantuan set. Some 500,000 feet of lumber, 250 tons of plaster, 25,000 pounds of nails, and 75 miles of reinforcing wire went into the structure. Twenty-one imposing plaster sphinxes, each weighing five tons, flanked a ceremonial roadway leading to the palace gates, where four 35-foot-high statues of Ramesses II stood guard.

A tent city named Camp De Mille arose near the set. Three thousand actors and 5,000 camels, cattle, horses, sheep, and pigs swarmed over the dunes. All of this cost $40,000 a day, a stupendous overhead by early Hollywood standards. De Mille worked with a tight shooting schedule against a backdrop of panicky telegrams from his boss, the legendary film mogul Adolph Zukor. "You have lost your mind. Stop filming and return to Los Angeles at once" was but one of them. But De Mille persisted, and he produced a triumphant epic.

A few days after the wrap, De Mille's huge set disappeared. Some of the sphinxes were carted away, others buried, and the palace facade was toppled over and buried. One of the largest movie sets ever built vanished under the dunes and was forgotten for 60 years. Then in 1983, documentary film maker Peter Brosnan and cinematographer Bruce Cardozo decided to follow up on De Mille's archaeological challenge. Did an ancient Egyptian city, albeit a twentieth-century one, lie under Guadalupe dunes? A long and painstaking search put them in touch with rancher Joe Gray, who had run cattle through the area for 40 years. Gray dimly remembered seeing the ruins of low walls. In June 1983, Brosnan stood on a large sand-covered mound overlooking the Pacific. He probed into the soft dune and uncovered part of a plaster horse's head. At this point Brosnan realized he needed expert assistance, so he contacted archaeologist Larry Wilcoxon of the University of California, Santa Barbara, who helped him map the site and locate more statuary. From this work came a blueprint for a scientific excavation that would form the centerpiece of a documentary on De Mille and *The Ten Commandments*. There was only one stumbling block: a proper dig would cost about $50,000. Brosnan recruited a team of archaeological advisers (I am one) and has been fundraising ever since.

Within days of the initial fundraising campaign, my telephone started ringing. Television stations, radio talk shows, *People* magazine, and dozens of newspapers put reporters on the story. We were interviewed by NBC Nightly News, talked on call-in radio shows in distant Australia, and received the ultimate compliment—coverage on the front page of *The Times* of London. Crank mail arrived from ten states.

Despite all this publicity and strong support from the Hollywood community and movie history buffs, it has taken six years to raise the first $10,000. Brosnan's benefactor is a financial institution, the Bank of America, an unusual source of funds for an archaeological undertaking. The bank's link to the project is due, in part, to De Mille himself. The famed filmmaker had once been a bank employee. Furthermore, the bank's founder, A. P. Giannini, had loaned money for the completion of *The Ten Commandments*. The first $10,000 has paid for a hi-tech search for subsurface features and for more preliminary survey work. This past November I watched as archaeologist John Parker of Parker and Associates in Morro Bay, California, laid out survey grids and mapped the exposed parts of the set. Parker and his team cleaned up and recorded about 226 square feet of plaster reliefs and statuary. Conservator Glen Wharton assessed potential conservation problems. Lambert Dolphin, a geophysicist, used ground-penetrating radar to explore the area where the avenue of sphinxes once stretched into the desert. Promising radar readings suggest that many of the sphinxes may still be in their original buried positions.

Under Parker's supervision, volunteers from the local Santa Maria Archaeological Society and Cuesta College made tests in the loose sand. Soon Brosnan was gazing at one of Ramesses' eyes. "That's the Pharaoh," he cried, his feelings no different from those of an archaeologist discovering a long-forgotten civilization or a spectacular royal tomb.

Most important of all, Parker's investigation revealed that the site is vanishing. The dune is moving at the rate of 3.8 feet a year, destroying it in the process. A third of the collapsed palace has already vanished. There will be nothing left by 2091.

Why dig a piece of Hollywood history where so much is already known about *The Ten Commandments*? "Does this not bring archaeology into disrepute?" one well-known archaeologist asked me querulously on the phone the other day. "Why excavate a site that is well known from contemporary photographs, artifacts, and drawings?" Above all, why divert funds to this "frivolous" project that could pay for "legitimate" research?

I must confess I have no sympathy for this viewpoint. First, *The Ten Commandments* set is the only surviving structure of its kind. On those grounds alone, it is worth serious attention. It would be naive to hope that the entire site can be saved, but a strong case can be made for recovering key artifacts for permanent preservation in such museums as the Smithsonian Institution, which have already expressed interest. Second, as many archaeologists who have visited the site have observed, the collapsed set is an extremely complicated assemblage of rubble, lumber, and metal that demands the most careful dissection if anything is to be learned of the construction of the set's palace. The loose sand and constant wind present unusual challenges for the stratigrapher, and an invaluable opportunity for training students. Third, Brosnan and his colleagues are movie historians,

156

whose primary objective is to make a documentary about Cecil B. De Mille and *The Ten Commandments*. The investigation of the set is part of a movie-making enterprise. The funds donated for excavation are, and will be, raised from sources that would not be available to other archaeological projects.

This excavation happened because a team of filmmakers, confronted with basically an archaeological problem, sought assistance from the scientific community when they needn't have. And that, to my mind, is a major step forward. Is not a modern ancient Egyptian palace an entirely legitimate target for archaeological exploration? Claims of "illegitimate archaeology" do nobody, least of all their perpetrators, any credit. ☀

GUIDE TO FURTHER READING

The references that follow will give you access to the detailed literature used to write each of the essays in the book. The works cited here have comprehensive bibliographies for the general reader and specialist alike and are relatively easy to find in academic, and sometimes public, libraries.

1. *Aping the Apes*

Blumenschine, Robert, and Cavallo, John. "Scavenging and Human Evolution," *Scientific American* 257 (10) (1992): 90–96.

Potts, Richard. "Home Bases and Early Hominids," *American Scientist* 72 (1984): 338–347.

2. *Elusive Homo Erectus*

Swisher, Carl, and others. "Age of the Earliest Known Hominids in Java, Indonesia," *Science* 263 (1994): 1118–1121.

3. *Prehistoric Artists*

Bahn, Paul, and Vertut, Jean. *Images of the Ice Age*. Viking, New York, 1988.

Lewis-Williams, David. *Seeing and Believing: Symbolic Meanings in Southern San Art*. Academic Press, Orlando, FL 1981.

4. *Reflections on the Kafue Flats*

Fagan, Brian, and Van Noten, Francis. *The Hunter-Gatherers of Gwisho*. Musée Royal de l'Afrique Centrale, Tervuren, Belgium, 1963.

Gould, Richard. *Living Archaeology*. Cambridge University Press, Cambridge, 1980.

5. *Precocious Fisherfolk*

Barnes, Gina. *China, Korea, and Japan*. Thames and Hudson, New York, 1993.

6. *Taming the Aurochs*

Smith, Andrew B. *Pastoralism in Africa*. Witwatersrand University Press, Johannesburg, 1992.

7. *Neolithic Newgrange*

O'Kelly, Michael J. *Newgrange*. Thames and Hudson, New York, 1993.

8. *New Finds at Flag Fen*

Pryor, Francis. *Flag Fen*. English Heritage, London, 1992.

9. *The Humbler Egyptians*

Kemp, Barry. *Ancient Egypt: The Anatomy of a Civilization*. Routledge, London, 1989.

10. *Saddle Up the Camels!*

Bulliet, Richard W. *The Camel and the Horse*. Harvard University Press, Cambridge, MA, 1975.

11. *Readers in Maya*

Schele, Linda, and Friedel, David. *Forest of Kings*. William Morrow, New York, 1991.

12. *Dating by Solar Eclipse*

Barnes, Gina. *China, Korea, and Japan*. Thames and Hudson, New York, 1993.

13. *The Magnificent Moche*

Alva, Walter, and Donnan, Christopher. *Royal Tombs of Sipán*. Fowler Museum of Cultural History, Los Angeles, CA, 1993.

14. *Brazil's Little Angola*

Orser, Charles, Jr. *In Search of Zumbi: Preliminary Archaeological Research at the Serra da Barriga, State of Algoas, Brazil.* Illinois State University, Normal, IL, 1992.

15. *Balsa Rafts to Ironclads*

Bass, George (ed.). *Ships and Shipwrecks of the Americas.* Thames and Hudson, New York, 1988.

16. *All About Eve*

Fagan, Brian. *The Journey from Eden.* Thames and Hudson, London, 1990.

Gamble, Clive. *Timewalkers.* Harvard University Press, Cambridge, MA, 1993.

17. *Tracking the First Americans*

Fagan, Brian. *The Great Journey.* Thames and Hudson, New York, 1987.

Meltzer, David. *Search for the First Americans.* Smithsonian Institution Press, Washington D.C., 1993.

18. *A Sexist View of Prehistory*

Gero, Joan M., and Conkey, Margaret W. (eds.). *Engendering Archaeology.* Basil Blackwell, Oxford, 1990.

Gimbutas, Marija. *Civilization of the Goddess.* HarperCollins, San Francisco, CA, 1991.

19. *A Case for Cannibalism*

White, T. D. *Prehistoric Cannibalism at Mancos 5MTUMR-2346.* Princeton University Press, Princeton, NJ, 1992.

20. *Teaching New Dogs Old Tricks*

Henderson, Richard. "Replicating Dog Travois Travel on the Northern Plains." *Plains Anthropologist* 39 (1994), 148: 145–159.

21. *The Arrogant Archaeologist*

Lynott, Mark J., and Wylie, Alison (eds.). *Ethics in American Archaeology: Challenges for the 1990s.* Society for American Archaeology, Washington D.C., 1995.

22. *Archaeology's Dirty Secret*

Lynott, Mark J. and Wylie, Alison (eds.). *Ethics in American Archaeology: Challenges for the 1990s.* Society for American Archaeology, Washington D.C., 1995.

23. *Black Day at Slack Farm*

Fagan, Brian. *Ancient North America.* 2nd ed. Thames and Hudson, New York, 1995.

24. *The Rose Affair*

Wainwright, G. J. "Saving the Rose." *Antiquity* 63 (1989), 240:430–436.

25. *Flooding the Maya Heartland*

Wilkerson, S. Jeffrey K. "Damming the Usumacinta: The Archaeological Impact." In M. G. Robinson (ed.). *Sixth Palenque Round Table, 1986.* University of Oklahoma Press, Norman, OK, 1986. 118–133.

26. *Enlightened Stewardship*

Messenger, Phyllis (ed.). *The Ethics of Collecting Cultural Property.* University of New Mexico Press, Albuquerque, NM, 1989.

27. *Detective Stories*

Blackburn, Thomas, and Hudson, Travis. *Time's Flotsam.* Ballena Press and Santa Barbara Museum of Natural History, Santa Barbara, CA, 1990.

28. *A Wanderer's Lament*

Macaulay, Rose. *The Pleasure of Ruins.* Thames and Hudson, London, 1964.

29. *Digging De Mille*

Orser, C.E., Jr., and Fagan, Brian. *Historical Archaeology*. HarperCollins, New York, 1995. ✸

CPSIA information can be obtained
at www.ICGtesting.com
Printed in the USA
LVHW04s1300290418
575305LV00002B/237/P

9 780761 991090